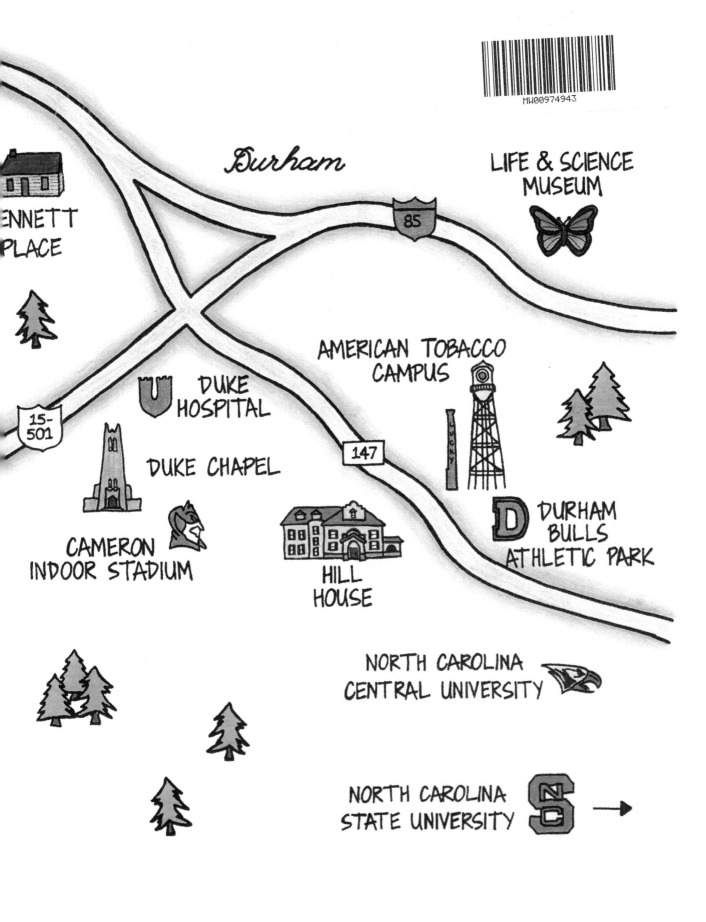

From the Junior League
of Durham and Orange Counties

Taste of Tobacco Road

A CULINARY JOURNEY ALONG THE FAMOUS NINE MILES

Foreword

By Sara Foster

I grew up in an era of Junior League cookbooks that taught home cooks how to cook, throw a party, and become great hostesses. From the punch at my sorority meetings to the casseroles we made for holidays, they were some of the most reliable cookbooks around. Most of them were handed down, well worn, and had a story behind them, like *River Road Recipes* (Baton Rouge, Louisiana) and *Come On In!* (Jackson, Mississippi). When I moved to New York and called my mother or grandmother for a recipe, they would give instructions like "add buttermilk until it looks like cornbread batter" or "stir in enough flour until it looks like cake batter." They never measured anything, and I was at a loss until I got my sister's torn and tattered copy of *River Road*. I loved it because all her favorite recipes were marked by splattered pages, and I knew these were recipes I could rely on. I felt as if I knew those cooks, was welcomed into their homes, and sat at their table. These are all things I tried to bring to Foster's Market when we opened in 1990.

Today's cooks focus on fresh, local, and healthy eating. Unlike the Junior League cookbooks I grew up with that used a can of this and a box of that, Junior League cookbooks have changed too. *Taste of Tobacco Road* is filled with recipes calling for fresh, seasonal ingredients that fit our lifestyle for easy, tasty, and nutritious meals. Like the past cookbooks of the Junior League of Durham and Orange Counties, *Carolina Thyme* and *Even More Special*, this book, too, will be dog-eared and splattered as time goes by and will be on your kitchen counter forever.

One of the things that drew me to the Durham-Chapel Hill area was the sense of community and the interest in fresh local food. There were a handful of great restaurants then—Magnolia Grill, Crooks Corner, La Residence, Parizade, and Fearrington—and a local health food store, Wellspring. The Carrboro Farmers' Market was one of the best I had ever seen and still is today, and the Durham Farmers' Market has grown to be equally as good. These farmers are the backbone of this community. They are the reason this area is populated with so many well-respected chefs, restaurateurs, and home cooks, and they have helped put us on the map as the "tastiest town in the South." Today, we are blessed to have many more great restaurants (too many to name) in both Durham and Chapel Hill, partly because of the dedication of local farmers and purveyors.

The Junior League of Durham and Orange Counties has been a part of this community much longer than Foster's Market, but we immediately became a part of their family. On any given day at Foster's, there is a meeting at the large table in the back to organize an event or fundraiser the JLDOC is planning. And one of those meetings was the beginning of this cookbook. As always, a dedicated committee had been selected to make this book the best, with over 200 recipes submitted, tested, and retested until each recipe was perfect. The favorite recipes from previous books were updated and added along with the best of some of the area's great chefs. Recipes from Junior League members that have been served to family and friends at dinner parties, family reunions, and cocktail parties over the years all make this book a winner.

When I spoke to Junior League president Jane Bullock, she was very passionate about the project. I remember what she said about one of the missions of the organization: "We try to teach women to think outside themselves and encourage them to use these skills to make a greater impact all around." This is also the way I try to teach people to cook: "Think outside the recipe, use it as a base and guideline, and make it your own." The recipes in this book are part of the local community and will become a collection for your everyday use. So I encourage all of you to use this book, make it your own, enjoy, and entertain.

Sara Foster is one of the country's most respected experts on simple, honest food prepared with fresh, local, and seasonal ingredients. Her approach to food is warm and relaxed, and she is a firm believer that any home cook can prepare fresh, flavorful home-cooked meals with comfort and simplicity. She is the founder and owner of Foster's Market, the cheerful, country-style market café in Durham, North Carolina. She is the author of five beloved and award-winning cookbooks: *Casual Cooking, The Foster's Market Cookbook, Fresh Every Day, Sara Foster's Southern Kitchen,* and *Foster's Market Favorites.* Sara previously worked as a chef for Martha Stewart's catering company, and she lives in Durham.

The Junior League of Durham and Orange Counties is proud to present our sponsoring partners in *Taste of Tobacco Road.*

Being involved in our communities is one of Belk's core values. The Junior League of Durham and Orange Counties represents one of the finest examples of community involvement in our area, and has been a great partner for several years.

We are happy to partner with the Junior League of Durham and Orange Counties to bring you these recipes that represent the best of our community. Personally, I can't wait to try the Sweet Potato and Salted Vanilla Caramel Bacon Cupcakes! We hope you try all of these recipes while surrounded by family and friends.

From our Belk family to yours,

Bill Roberts

Chairman, Belk Northern Division

Gold Level Sponsors

THE CAROLINA INN

EST. 1924

Silver Level Sponsors

Alivia's Durham Bistro	Parizade
Carolina Brewery	Piedmont Restaurant
Firebirds Wood Fired Grill	Refectory Cafe
Mad Hatter Bakeshop & Cafe	Saladelia Cafe

Bronze Level Sponsors

Betsy's Cheese Straws	Local Yogurt
Chapel Hill Toffee	The Crunkleton
He's Not Here	

Introduction

The Junior League of Durham and Orange Counties is pleased to present this new cookbook: *Taste of Tobacco Road*. Just like the diverse recipes you will find within this book, we represent women from all backgrounds and traditions, with different life experiences.

At the core, we are a group of women who want to make a difference in our community. I, along with presidents Lauren Dickerson (2013–14) and Kate Rugani (2014–15), want to thank the cookbook committee, the JLDOC Board of Directors, our membership, and our community partners for their collaboration on this book.

We started this journey several years ago, thinking that the process of creating a new cookbook would bring our membership together, and it did. We listened to our older members and heard the stories of how past cookbooks were created, and then included a few of our favorite past cookbook recipes within these pages. We met new members and found out more about who they are and what skills they bring. We shared thoughts about our families, our personal lives, and our passion for helping those around us. We shared more than just food; we shared hope for the future of our community.

Each of our projects, like the recipes in this cookbook, begins with a group of women who had an idea to do something great. It takes different ingredients—in just the right amount; it requires planning and attention—to whisk, to blend, and to bring it all together. And, finally, we present something amazing that brings people together.

Every day, the JLDOC lives by our mission to develop the potential of women, promote voluntarism, and improve our community. We are committed to providing training and support to every League member to develop the talents and skills necessary to make a real difference in Durham and Orange Counties. Our goal is to create and develop programs like our Healthy Living Initiative, which will create lasting change and make a difference in the lives of those who live in our community.

I hope you will enjoy following these recipes down "Tobacco Road," which will lead you to learn more about the heart and work of the women of the Junior League of Durham and Orange Counties.

Thank you for bringing JLDOC to your table.

Best regards,

Jane Bullock

JLDOC President, 2012–13 and 2015–16

Table of Contents

Taste the Beginnings

What Is Tobacco Road?

The real *Tobacco Road* is difficult to find on a map—and many would argue that it doesn't even physically exist. There are many roads named *Tobacco Road* scattered throughout the state of North Carolina, some even near Durham and Chapel Hill. But these roads aren't *The Tobacco Road* of which everyone speaks today; the real *Tobacco Road* can only be found on the grassy fields and hardwood floors here in the North Carolina Piedmont.

Before becoming associated with North Carolina, *Tobacco Road* was the title of a book about sharecroppers in Georgia. But North Carolina, not Georgia, was the center of the tobacco industry long before the novel was written, and it was the remarkably compact area in North Carolina's Piedmont region that came to be called *Tobacco Road*.

The four universities in this area (Duke, UNC, NCCU, and NC State) are separated by no more than twenty-five miles. The proximity of these schools has not only created a diverse and educated population, but also a natural rivalry between students, faculty, fans, and alumni that many sportscasters refer to as *Tobacco Road*.

As for the "famous" nine miles? You won't find that on a map. This is the straight distance between Durham and Chapel Hill, or, to sports fans, the stretch between Duke University and the University of North Carolina—close enough that a parachute jumper once actually descended into the wrong stadium on game day, much to the surprise of the fans. It is the regional phenomenon that has created one of the most intense rivalries in men's college basketball and has also credited Duke and UNC as being the true heart of *The Tobacco Road*.

Caprese Salad Pops

30 cherry tomatoes (about 3 pints)
15 basil leaves, torn into halves and folded
30 fresh mozzarella cheese balls (about 1 pound), drained, or 30 mozzarella cubes
1/2 cup aged balsamic vinegar
Freshly cracked pepper to taste

Rinse the tomatoes and pat dry. Thread the tomatoes, basil and cheese in the order given onto extra-large wooden picks. Arrange the salad pops on a platter. Bring the vinegar to a boil in a small saucepan. Cook until reduced to the consistency of syrup, stirring constantly and watching carefully to ensure that the vinegar does not burn. Drizzle over the salad pops. Sprinkle with cracked pepper.

Yield: 30 salad pops

Baked Brie Bites

2 (15-count) packages frozen mini phyllo shells
Nonstick cooking spray
1 (8-ounce) round Brie cheese
1 jar fruit preserves, such as seedless red raspberry preserves

Thaw the phyllo shells for 10 minutes. Arrange the shells on a foil-lined baking sheet sprayed with nonstick cooking spray. Remove the rind from the cheese using a sharp knife. Cut the cheese into 1/2-inch cubes and place a cube in each phyllo cup. Top each with 1/2 teaspoon of the preserves. Bake at 350 degrees for 8 to 10 minutes or until the cheese is melted.

NOTE: The best way to buy the freshest Brie is by feel. Choose the softest cheese.

Yield: 30 bites

Fresh Bruschetta

1 French baguette or similar Italian bread
1/4 cup extra-virgin olive oil
6 or 7 ripe tomatoes
2 teaspoons balsamic vinegar
2 cloves of garlic, minced
1 tablespoon extra-virgin olive oil
10 to 12 fresh basil leaves, chopped
Salt and freshly ground black pepper to taste

Cut the baguette into 16 slices and arrange on a baking sheet. Brush the slices with 1/4 cup olive oil. Bake at 425 degrees for 5 to 8 minutes. Turn the slices over and bake until toasted. Seed the tomatoes and cut into 1/4-inch cubes. Combine the tomatoes, vinegar, garlic, 1 tablespoon olive oil, basil, salt and pepper in a bowl and mix well. Spoon over the toasts.

NOTE: To add a summertime twist to this classic, try adding crumbled fresh goat cheese.

Yield: 16 toasts

Roquefort Grapes

16 ounces cream cheese, softened
6 ounces Roquefort or blue cheese, crumbled
2 to 3 cups pecan halves, finely chopped
4 to 5 dozen seedless red grapes (about 1/2 to 3/4 pound)

Combine the cream cheese and Roquefort cheese in a mixing bowl. Beat until smooth.

Toast the pecans in a skillet over medium heat for 3 minutes, stirring constantly. Spoon into a shallow bowl to cool.

Rinse the grapes; drain and pat dry. Shape 1 to 2 teaspoons of the cheese mixture around each grape. Roll in the pecans to coat. Arrange on a serving platter. Chill until serving time.

Yield: 4 to 5 dozen

Southern Cheese Straws

1 pound sharp Cheddar cheese, chilled
1 pound butter, softened
4 cups all-purpose flour
1 teaspoon salt
1/4 teaspoon (about) cayenne pepper

Grate the cheese into a mixing bowl. Let stand until the cheese comes to room temperature. Add the butter. Beat with an electric mixer until thoroughly mixed. Sift in the flour, salt and cayenne pepper gradually, beating well after each addition. Pipe 5- to 6-inch straws through a cookie press onto baking sheets. Bake at 325 degrees for 20 to 25 minutes.

NOTE: May also shape the dough into small balls and flatten with a fork or roll out on a floured surface and cut into rounds.

Yield: 5 dozen

Creamy Chicken Puffs

3 whole boneless skinless chicken breasts, cut into halves
1/4 cup vegetable oil
1/2 teaspoon garlic salt
1/4 teaspoon dried rosemary
1 (6-count) package frozen pastry shells, thawed
3 ounces cream cheese with chives, cut into 6 portions, softened

Cook the chicken breasts briefly in the oil in a skillet to start the cooking process; do not brown. Sprinkle with the garlic salt and rosemary. Roll out each pastry shell into a 7- to 9-inch circle. Place a chicken breast half on the bottom half of each pastry circle. Spread each with 1 portion of the cream cheese. Fold pastry over each chicken breast; seal the edges. Arrange on a baking sheet. Place in a 450-degree oven; reduce heat immediately to 400 degrees. Bake, uncovered, for 30 minutes or until golden brown.

Yield: 6 servings

Spicy Deviled Eggs

12 hard-cooked eggs, cooled and shelled
3 1/2 tablespoons mayonnaise
2 teaspoons Dijon mustard
2 teaspoons white vinegar
1/4 teaspoon kosher salt
1/8 teaspoon pepper
4 dashes of Tabasco sauce, or to taste
1 teaspoon chopped pickled jalapeños, drained
1 teaspoon finely chopped pimentos, drained
1 teaspoon chopped parsley
1 teaspoon finely chopped chives
Paprika and fresh jalapeño slice halves for garnish

Cut the eggs lengthwise into halves using a sharp knife. Remove the egg yolks using a small spoon and place in a small mixing bowl. Place the egg whites cut sides up on a serving plate. Mash the egg yolks in a bowl using a fork until the texture of loose crumbs. Add the mayonnaise, mustard, vinegar, salt, pepper and Tabasco sauce; mix until smooth. Combine the pickled jalapeños, pimentos, parsley and chives in a small bowl and mix well. Fold into the egg yolk mixture. Spoon into a piping bag or a resealable plastic bag with an end snipped. Fill the egg whites in a circular pattern. Garnish with paprika and fresh jalapeños.

VARIATION: For a prettier presentation, mix the mashed egg yolks with the mayonnaise, mustard, vinegar, salt, pepper and Tabasco sauce in a bowl. Pipe into the egg whites in a circular pattern. Top each with a mixture of pickled jalapeños, pimentos, parsley, chives and a dash of sunflower oil. Garnish with paprika and fresh jalapeños.

Yield: 24 servings

DEVILED VS. ANGEL

Food-based references to the term *deviled* date back to the eighteenth century; the first known printing of the description was in 1786. It was in the nineteenth century, though, that the term came to mean spicy or zesty food, including egg yolks prepared with mustard, pepper, or other ingredients and stuffed into the egg white.

In parts of the South, the terms stuffed eggs, salad eggs, dressed eggs, or angel eggs are also used, particularly when served in connection with church functions, avoiding the term devil. The term *angel eggs* is often used in association with eggs stuffed with "healthier" alternatives.

Christmas Log with Pattie Crackers

from Edgar Higgins, Original Voice of the Duke Blue Devils

The original "Voice of the Blue Devils" from 1940 to the mid-1980s, Ed Higgins announced for Duke University basketball and football. Originally from Asheville, Ed relocated after World War II to Durham, where he met his wife, Helen, and quickly adopted her love for entertaining in the height of the home house party.

PATTIE CRACKERS

3 ounces cream cheese, softened
1/2 cup butter, softened

1 cup all-purpose flour
1/2 teaspoon salt

CHRISTMAS LOG

12 ounces feta cheese, crumbled
1 cup unsalted butter
8 ounces cream cheese, softened
2 cloves of garlic, finely minced
1 shallot, finely minced

3 tablespoons good-quality dry vermouth
White pepper to taste
1 cup chopped sundried tomatoes
1/2 cup pine nuts, toasted
3/4 cup pesto

For the Pattie Crackers, combine the cream cheese, butter, flour and salt in a bowl and mix well. Shape into a ball. Break off walnut-size balls or roll to 1/4-inch thickness and cut into squares. Press each ball or square into a mini muffin cup. Bake at 325 degrees for 15 to 20 minutes or until light brown. Let stand to cool. May be frozen; cover with foil and reheat at a low oven temperature.

For the Christmas Log, combine the feta cheese, butter, cream cheese, garlic, shallot, vermouth and white pepper in a food processor and process until smooth. Line an oiled gelatin mold or medium bowl with plastic wrap. Layer half of the sundried tomatoes, pine nuts, pesto and feta cheese mixture in the mold in the order given. Repeat the layers and pat down into the mold. Chill, covered, for 1 hour or longer, or optimally overnight. Invert onto a serving plate; remove the plastic wrap. Serve with the Pattie Crackers.

Yield: 15 servings

Sweet-and-Sour Meatballs

from Woody Durham, Longtime Voice of the UNC Tar Heels

"The Voice of the Tar Heels," Woody Durham was the longtime sports radio announcer for football and men's basketball at the University of North Carolina at Chapel Hill. He and his wife, Jean, like to keep these meatballs in the freezer to reheat as a quick cocktail appetizer—just in time for the big game.

SWEET-AND-SOUR SAUCE

1 cup sugar
3/4 cup apple cider vinegar
3/4 cup water
1 teaspoon paprika

1/2 teaspoon salt
2 tablespoons cornstarch
1 tablespoon cold water

MEATBALLS

3/4 pound lean ground beef
1/4 pound ground pork
3/4 cup rolled oats
1/2 cup milk
1/4 cup finely chopped water chestnuts

1 tablespoon Worcestershire sauce
1/2 teaspoon onion salt
1/2 teaspoon garlic salt
Dash of hot red pepper sauce

For the Sweet-and-Sour Sauce, combine the sugar, vinegar, 3/4 cup water, paprika and salt in a saucepan. Cook over medium heat for 5 minutes, stirring frequently. Blend the cornstarch and 1 tablespoon water in a small bowl to make a slurry. Add to the sauce and mix well. Cook just until the mixture is thickened, stirring frequently.

For the Meatballs, combine the ground beef, ground pork, oats, milk, water chestnuts, Worcestershire sauce, onion salt, garlic salt and hot sauce in a large bowl; mix well. Shape into 1-inch balls. Place in a rimmed baking pan. Bake at 375 degrees for 20 minutes, turning the meatballs after 10 minutes. Remove the meatballs to a serving dish using a slotted spoon. Add the Sweet-and-Sour Sauce and stir gently to coat. May freeze in a freezer-proof container. Thaw and reheat the meatballs and sauce. May also serve over rice as an entrée.

Yield: 2 dozen

Crab-Stuffed Mushrooms

36 baby portabella or shiitake mushrooms
4 tablespoons butter
2 green onions, chopped
8 ounces cream cheese, softened
1/2 cup light mayonnaise
1/4 cup shredded Parmigiano-Reggiano cheese
8 ounces fresh crabmeat
2 cloves of garlic, minced
Salt, pepper and Old Bay seasoning to taste
3 tablespoons minced parsley
3 tablespoons shredded Parmigiano-Reggiano cheese

Remove the stems from the mushrooms. Mince the mushroom stems and sauté in the butter in a skillet. Add the onions. Cook for 5 to 8 minutes or until golden brown. Combine the cream cheese, mayonnaise, 1/4 cup cheese, crabmeat, garlic, salt, pepper, Old Bay seasoning and parsley in a bowl; mix well. Stir in the mushroom stems. Chill for 20 minutes.

Hollow out the mushroom caps to make space for the crabmeat filling. Spoon the filling into the mushroom caps. Arrange on a baking sheet. Sprinkle with 3 tablespoons cheese. Bake at 375 degrees for 12 to 15 minutes or until the tops are golden brown and the cheese is melted. Serve warm.

Yield: 36 servings

Baked Mussels with Butter, Cheese and Garlic

These can be made earlier in the day and stored in the refrigerator until ready to bake.

36 frozen mussels on the half shell
1 cup grated sharp Cheddar cheese
3 large cloves of garlic

2 tablespoons butter
2 tablespoons olive oil

Place the mussels shell side down on a baking sheet. Combine the cheese, garlic, butter and olive oil in a food processor. Pulse to make a paste. Spoon 1/2 teaspoon of the cheese mixture on top of each mussel. Bake at 400 degrees for 15 minutes or until the topping is lightly browned. Serve warm.

NOTE: This dish is also exquisite with freshly steamed mussels. For a fresh mussel alternative, wash and clean the mussels thoroughly. Steam for 2 to 3 minutes or just until the shells begin to open, discarding any that do not open. Remove the top shell and beard of the mussel. Prepare and bake as directed.

Yield: 36 mussels

Lemon Dill Grilled Oysters

1/4 cup buttermilk
2 small cloves of garlic, grated
2 tablespoons chopped fresh dill leaves
1 tablespoon minced fresh parsley leaves
1 tablespoon finely grated lemon zest

2 teaspoons fresh lemon juice
1 cup mayonnaise
1 to 2 dozen tightly closed fresh oysters
  in the shell

Combine the buttermilk, garlic, dill and parsley in a food processor. Process until smooth. Combine with the lemon zest, lemon juice and mayonnaise in a bowl; mix well. Chill in the refrigerator. The sauce will thicken as it chills.

Shuck the oysters, leaving the meat in the deeper shell. Place shell side down on oiled grill grates over an even layer of white-hot coals. Grill for 5 to 8 minutes. Bathe the oysters with the sauce. Serve immediately with crackers and the remaining sauce.

Yield: 1 to 2 dozen

Brie Pizza with Sage and Pine Nuts

1 ball of store-bought pizza dough
2 tablespoons olive oil
Salt and pepper to taste
1 medium round of Brie cheese, cut into slices
1 cup toasted pine nuts
1 bunch fresh sage leaves
2 tablespoons olive oil

Roll out the pizza dough into an oval on a greased baking sheet. Brush the dough with 2 tablespoons olive oil and sprinkle with salt and pepper. Arrange the cheese evenly over the pizza dough. Sprinkle with the pine nuts and sage. Bake at 400 degrees for 20 minutes or until the crust is lightly browned and the cheese is melted. Drizzle 2 tablespoons olive oil over the pizza.

NOTE: Substitute any fresh herbs you have on hand and make in any season.

Yield: 6 to 8 servings

Fresh Zucchini Pizzas

1 large zucchini, cut into 1/2-inch slices
8 ounces prepared spaghetti sauce
Grated Monterey Jack cheese and grated Parmesan cheese to taste
Sliced black olives and minced green onions to taste
Garlic salt to taste
Freshly ground pepper to taste
Chopped fresh oregano or dried oregano to taste

Arrange the zucchini slices on a baking sheet. Top each with a small amount of spaghetti sauce. Sprinkle with the Monterey Jack cheese, Parmesan cheese, olives and green onions. Season with garlic salt, pepper and oregano. Broil until bubbly. Serve immediately.

Yield: 12 to 16 bite-size pizzas

Chilled Veggie Pizza

2 packages refrigerator crescent roll dough
1 cup mayonnaise
8 ounces cream cheese, softened
1/3 cup powdered buttermilk
2 tablespoons dried parsley
2 teaspoons garlic powder
2 teaspoons dried onion flakes
1 1/2 teaspoons dried dill weed
1 teaspoon dried chives
1 teaspoon salt
1 teaspoon ground black pepper
Chopped fresh broccoli, shredded carrots, sliced fresh mushrooms and
    sliced black olives to taste
Shredded Cheddar cheese and mozzarella cheese to taste

Roll out each crescent roll dough on a floured surface to 1/4-inch thickness. Place on baking sheets. Bake according to the package directions; cool. Combine the mayonnaise, cream cheese, powdered buttermilk, parsley, garlic powder, onion flakes, dill weed, chives, salt and pepper in a mixing bowl. Beat until smooth. Spread over the baked crescent roll crusts. Sprinkle with broccoli, carrots, mushrooms, olives, Cheddar cheese and mozzarella cheese. Bake at 350 degrees for 10 minutes or just until the cheese is melted.

NOTE: You may add any chopped fresh seasonal vegetables to the toppings.

Yield: 12 to 16 servings

Caviar Pie

Although the price of caviar may seem prohibitive, this dressy hors d'oeuvres makes a little go a long way.

6 hard-cooked eggs, finely chopped
3 tablespoons mayonnaise
6 scallions, finely chopped
8 ounces cream cheese, softened
2/3 cup sour cream
1 (3-ounce) jar black lumpfish caviar
Thin lemon wedges, parsley sprigs and sieved egg yolks for garnish

Combine the eggs and mayonnaise in a small bowl and mix well. Spread over the bottom of a greased 8-inch springform pan. Sprinkle with the scallions. Beat the cream cheese and sour cream in a mixing bowl for 3 minutes or until smooth. Spread evenly over the scallions. Chill, covered with plastic wrap, for 3 hours or longer.

Sprinkle with the caviar. Loosen the side with a knife; remove the band from the pan. Garnish with lemon wedges, parsley sprigs and sieved egg yolks. Serve with party pumpernickel bread or crackers.

NOTE: If doubling the recipe, use a 10-inch springform pan.

Yield: 10 to 12 servings

Seven-Layer Greek Dip

8 ounces cream cheese, softened
3 cloves of garlic, minced or pressed
2 teaspoons lemon juice
1 teaspoon dried dill weed or Greek seasoning
1 1/2 cups hummus
1 cup seeded diced cucumber
1 cup seeded diced tomatoes
1/2 cup chopped Kalamata olives
1/3 cups chopped green onions
1/2 cup crumbled feta cheese
2 to 4 tablespoons minced fresh parsley

Combine the cream cheese, garlic, lemon juice and dill weed in a mixing bowl. Beat until light and fluffy. Spread over the bottom of a pie plate or a small shallow baking dish. Spread the hummus over the cream cheese mixture. Layer with the cucumber, tomatoes, olives, green onions, feta cheese and parsley. Chill, covered with plastic wrap, for 2 hours or longer. Serve with pita chips, fresh vegetables and/or flatbread for dipping.

Yield: 7 cups

Savory Baked Crab Dip

16 ounces cream cheese
1/2 small onion, finely minced
1 1/2 tablespoons prepared horseradish
1 clove of garlic, minced
1 tablespoon sherry (optional)

1 tablespoon Worcestershire sauce
1 teaspoon hot red pepper sauce
Salt and pepper to taste
12 ounces local lump crab meat
Grated Parmesan cheese to taste

Heat the cream cheese in a saucepan over low heat just until melted. Stir in the onion, horseradish, garlic, sherry, Worcestershire sauce, hot sauce, salt, pepper and crabmeat. Spoon into a baking dish. Sprinkle generously with cheese. Bake at 400 degrees for 30 minutes or until golden brown and bubbly. Serve with warm pita points.

Yield: 4 cups

Elegant Olive Dip

8 ounces low-fat cream cheese, softened
1/2 cup real mayonnaise
1/2 cup chopped black olives

1/2 cup chopped green olives
2 tablespoons green olive juice
1/4 to 1/2 cup chopped pecans

Combine the cream cheese and mayonnaise in a mixing bowl; beat until blended. Add the black olives, green olives, olive juice and pecans; mix well. Spoon into a serving dish. Chill for 2 hours or longer. Serve with crackers and vegetable sticks.

Yield: 2 1/2 cups

Nana's Pimento Cheese

16 ounces cream cheese
1 1/2 to 1 cup mayonnaise
1 pound sharp Cheddar cheese, shredded
1 pound extra-sharp white Cheddar cheese, shredded
1 large jar pimentos, drained
1 teaspoon smoked hot paprika or regular paprika

Combine the cream cheese, mayonnaise, sharp Cheddar cheese, white Cheddar cheese, pimentos and paprika in a large bowl; mix gently. Chill, covered, until serving time. Serve in sandwiches or with crackers. Best served at room temperature.

Yield: about 6 cups

Chipotle Pimento Cheese

6 ounces sharp Cheddar cheese, coarsely grated
4 ounces extra-sharp Cheddar cheese, coarsely grated
4 ounces smoked Gouda, coarsely grated
1 can chipotle peppers in adobo sauce
1 large roasted red pepper
1 tablespoon stone-ground mustard
3 tablespoons mayonnaise
Black pepper to taste

Combine the sharp Cheddar cheese, extra-sharp Cheddar cheese and Gouda in a medium mixing bowl. Drain the chipotle peppers, reserving 2 teaspoons of the adobo sauce. Dice 1 chipotle pepper finely, reserving the remaining peppers for another use. Dice the roasted red pepper finely and pat dry. Add the chipotle pepper and red pepper to the cheeses. Stir in the mustard, mayonnaise and reserved adobo sauce. Beat for 5 minutes or until creamy. Season with pepper to taste. Serve at room temperature.

Yield: about 3 cups

PIMENTO CHEESE

In any Southern home, pimento cheese is as much of a staple as peanut butter. It's the perfect topping for anything from celery sticks to hamburgers and has gone quite mainstream in the past few years. What used to be an affordable sandwich in the 1920s, due to an abundance of pimentos grown in the south and the low cost of cheese, is now showing up on the menus of the finest Tobacco Road restaurants. It's the "caviar of the South."

Black Bean Salsa

3 to 4 cans black beans, rinsed and drained
1 can niblet corn, drained
1 red bell pepper, diced
1 yellow or orange bell pepper, diced
1 can chopped green chilies, drained
1 can diced tomatoes, drained
1 bunch scallions, chopped
1 jalapeño pepper, finely chopped
1 bunch fresh cilantro, chopped
1 tablespoon chopped fresh oregano (optional)
1 tablespoon cumin
2/3 cup olive oil
1/3 cup red wine vinegar
Salt and pepper to taste

Combine the beans, corn, bell peppers, green chilies, tomatoes, scallions, jalapeño, cilantro, oregano and cumin in a large bowl. Whisk the olive oil and vinegar together in a small bowl. Add to the vegetable mixture and mix gently. Season with salt and pepper. Serve with tortilla chips.

NOTE: For a milder salsa, remove the seeds from the jalapeño.

Yield: about 7 to 9 cups

Three-Berry Salsa with Cinnamon Sugar Tortilla Chips

STRAWBERRIES AND BLUEBERRIES

In 2001, North Carolina designated strawberries and blueberries as the state's official berries. Each spring, it's traditional for families to pick their own berries at local farms throughout the state. To care for fresh berries, keep them dry, washing only when ready to use. If the berries are refrigerated, bring them to room temperature before serving to enhance their natural flavors.

CINNAMON SUGAR TORTILLA CHIPS

4 small flour tortillas
Nonstick cooking spray
2 tablespoons sugar
1 teaspoon ground cinnamon

THREE-BERRY SALSA

1 pint fresh strawberries, hulled and chopped
1 small package fresh blueberries, chopped
1 package blackberries, chopped
1 Red Delicious apple, chopped (optional)
1/4 cup sugar
1/4 cup fresh lemon juice
1/4 teaspoon ground cinnamon
1/4 teaspoon nutmeg
1 large banana, chopped

For the Cinnamon Sugar Tortilla Chips, cut each tortilla into 8 triangles; coat with nonstick cooking spray. Place on a baking sheet. Sprinkle with a mixture of the sugar and cinnamon. Bake at 350 degrees for 6 to 8 minutes or until lightly browned; cool completely.

For the Three-Berry Salsa, combine the strawberries, blueberries, blackberries and apple in a bowl. Add the sugar, lemon juice, cinnamon and nutmeg; mix well. Add the banana just before serving.

Yield: 32 servings

Chicken Cheese Ball

1/3 cup powdered buttermilk
2 tablespoons dried parsley
1 1/2 teaspoons dried dill weed
2 teaspoons garlic powder
2 teaspoons onion powder
2 teaspoons onion flakes

1 teaspoon each salt and pepper
1 teaspoon dried chives
16 ounces cream cheese, softened
12 1/2 ounces shredded roasted chicken
1 1/2 to 2 cups shredded Cheddar cheese
1 1/2 cups chopped pecans, crushed

Combine the powdered buttermilk, parsley, dill weed, garlic powder, onion powder, onion flakes, salt, pepper and chives in a small bowl and mix well. Combine the cream cheese, chicken and Cheddar cheese in a large bowl and mix well. Add the buttermilk mixture and mix well. Shape into a ball. Coat with the pecans. Wrap the cheese ball in plastic wrap and then aluminum foil. Chill overnight. Serve with assorted crackers.

NOTE: The chicken can be omitted to make a vegetarian cheese ball.

Yield: 16 to 24 servings

Herbed Boursin

16 ounces cream cheese, softened
8 ounces whipped unsalted butter,
    at room temperature
1 clove of garlic, mashed
1/4 teaspoon pepper

1/4 teaspoon each dried oregano, thyme,
    marjoram, dill weed and basil
Coarsely ground black pepper,
    sweet Hungarian paprika or
    poppy seeds to taste (optional)

Beat the cream cheese and butter in a mixing bowl until smooth and blended. Add the garlic, pepper, oregano, thyme, marjoram, dill weed and basil; mix well. Shape into a ball or log, or spoon into ramekins. Chill until firm. Roll in or sprinkle with the coarsely ground black pepper, Hungarian paprika or poppy seeds. Chill until serving time. Soften for 10 minutes before serving. Serve with mild-tasting crackers.

NOTE: This recipe may be easily cut in half.

Yield: 10 to 12 servings

Country Ham Rolls

1 1/2 cups chopped onions
5 1/3 tablespoons butter, melted
2 tablespoons Dijon mustard
1 tablespoon Worcestershire sauce
1 foil pan of dinner rolls
1 pound thinly sliced country ham
1 package sliced Swiss cheese
Poppy seeds

Combine the onions, butter, mustard and Worcestershire sauce in a bowl and mix well.

Cut the rolls horizontally into halves using a serrated knife. Remove the top layer of rolls in one piece. Spread the onion mixture over the bottom layer. Layer with the ham and cheese. Replace the top layer.

Brush with additional melted butter and sprinkle with poppy seeds. Bake at 350 degrees for 45 minutes or until the cheese is melted and the rolls are heated through.

Yield: 12 to 16 servings

HOGS AND PIGS

Hogs and pigs have historically been an important part of North Carolina agriculture, and the industry has grown dramatically in recent years. Many farmers who had formerly tended other crops, such as tobacco, have turned to hog farming.

Oyster Cracker Tidbits

10 ounces (about 6 cups) oyster crackers
1 envelope ranch dressing mix
1/2 teaspoon dried dill weed
1/4 teaspoon lemon pepper
1/4 teaspoon garlic salt
1/4 cup vegetable oil

Combine the oyster crackers, ranch dressing mix, dill weed, lemon pepper and garlic salt in a large bowl and mix gently. Drizzle the oil over the top, stirring from the bottom of the bowl to mix well. Store in an airtight container.

NOTE: These crackers will stay fresh for several weeks.

Yield: 6 cups

Taste the Tradition

BRUNCH

Schools of Tobacco Road

Long before Duke, North Carolina State, and North Carolina Central became universities, the University of North Carolina at Chapel Hill admitted its first student in 1796. UNC was the largest university in the South before the Civil War, and is one of three universities to hold the title of the "oldest public university in the United States." The school, which covers 729 acres in the town of Chapel Hill, is often referred to as "Carolina" to signify its oldest collegiate title in the Carolinas.

The school that would become Duke University began as Brown's Schoolhouse 1838. It would transition through numerous name changes over the years and even a location change from Randolph County, North Carolina, to Durham. Named Trinity College in 1859 due to the support from the Methodist Church, the school moved to Durham and was renamed Duke University in 1924, when James B. Duke established the Duke Endowment Fund and gave the school $19 million.

Twenty miles to the east, another rival was growing. In 1887, North Carolina College of Agriculture and Mechanical Arts was founded in Raleigh, the state's capital. Adding schools of engineering, textiles, design, humanities, and physical and social sciences through the years, it is known today as North Carolina State University.

North Carolina College, a public historically African-American university, was also in development at this time. Becoming a state-funded university in 1923, the college's first four-year class graduated in 1929 and went on to earn accreditation in 1937. North Carolina College at Durham became North Carolina Central University in 1969. Today, NCSU is part of the UNC system and is acclaimed for top programs in criminal justice, business administration, and law.

Honey Pecan Granola

3 cups rolled oats
1 cup shredded coconut
1 cup chopped pecans
1 cup raisins
1/2 cup local honey
1/2 cup butter

Combine the oats, coconut, pecans and raisins in a large bowl. Combine the honey and butter in a small saucepan. Cook over low heat until the butter is melted, stirring frequently. Pour over the oats mixture, tossing to mix. Spread the granola on a parchment-lined baking sheet. Bake at 300 degrees for 30 minutes. Toss the mixture with a fork to crumble. Bake for 10 to 15 minutes longer or until browned, tossing occasionally. Let the granola cool on the baking sheet. Store in an airtight container.

NOTE: May substitute any nuts or dried fruit for the pecans and raisins. The key is to use local honey!

Yield: 6 cups

HONEY

Honeybees are the state insects of North Carolina, and they play an important role in our agricultural economy. One-third of the fruits and vegetables we eat depend on honeybees for pollination. These social and cooperative insects live together in colonies. Honey, which honeybees produce to feed the colony, is a natural sweetener, and it is the only food produced by insects that is eaten by human beings. It is also the only food that never spoils. Honey contains all the substances needed to sustain life: water, vitamins, minerals, and enzymes. Talk about a super food!

Baked Apple French Toast

Sylvia Hatchell is the head coach of the women's basketball team at the University of North Carolina at Chapel Hill and holds the record for the most wins in NCAA women's basketball history. This recipe was one of Coach Hatchell's favorites during her fight with leukemia. The Tobacco Road community has a longstanding tradition of rallying around our own during their personal trials. Down here, we believe that our trials unite us and that food can serve as a comfort and an energy booster, both mentally and physically.

20 (1-inch-thick) slices French bread
1 (21-ounce) can apple pie filling
8 eggs
2 cups 2-percent milk
2 teaspoons vanilla extract
1/2 teaspoon ground cinnamon
1/2 teaspoon ground nutmeg
1/2 cup cold butter, cut into cubes
1 cup packed brown sugar
1 cup chopped pecans
2 tablespoons corn syrup

Arrange 10 slices of the bread in a greased 9×13-inch baking dish. Spread the pie filling over the bread. Arrange the remaining bread over the pie filling. Whisk the eggs lightly in a medium bowl. Add the milk, vanilla, cinnamon and nutmeg; whisk lightly. Pour over the bread. Chill, covered, overnight. Let stand at room temperature for 30 minutes before baking. Cut the butter into the brown sugar in a small bowl until crumbly. Stir in the pecans and corn syrup. Sprinkle over the bread. Bake at 350 degrees for 35 to 40 minutes or until a knife inserted in the center comes out clean. Serve with warm maple syrup if desired.

Yield: 10 servings

Strawberries and Cream French Toast

1 loaf French bread, sliced on the diagonal
8 ounces cream cheese, softened
6 eggs
2 cups milk
1/2 teaspoon vanilla extract
1/4 teaspoon ground nutmeg
Strawberry jam or preserves
Confectioners' sugar

Spread half the bread slices with the cream cheese. Top with the remaining bread slices. Arrange in a buttered 9 x 13-inch baking dish. Combine the eggs, milk, vanilla and nutmeg in a mixing bowl. Whisk until thoroughly mixed. Pour over the bread. Chill, covered with foil, overnight.

Remove the foil and place the baking dish in an unheated oven. Set oven temperature to 350 degrees. Bake for 45 minutes or until puffed and browned. Top with strawberry jam and sprinkle with confectioners' sugar.

Yield: 8 servings

Grandma's Coffee Cake

1/2 cup butter, melted
2 cups sugar
2 eggs
2 cups all-purpose flour
2 teaspoons ground cinnamon

2 teaspoons baking powder
1 teaspoon salt
1 cup milk
Nonstick cooking spray

Combine the butter, sugar and eggs in a large mixing bowl; mix well. Mix the flour, cinnamon, baking powder and salt in a small bowl. Add the flour mixture to the butter mixture alternately with the milk, whisking to remove any lumps after each addition. Pour into two 8- or 9-inch square or round baking pans sprayed with nonstick cooking spray. Bake at 350 degrees for 30 to 35 minutes or until golden brown.

Yield: 12 servings

Game Day Breakfast Casserole

1 tablespoon butter, softened
6 to 8 slices cinnamon swirl bread
10 slices crisp-cooked bacon, crumbled
2 cups crumbled cooked sausage
1 cup shredded sharp Cheddar cheese
8 medium eggs, lightly beaten
2 cups milk
1 teaspoon salt
1 1/2 teaspoons dry mustard
1/2 teaspoon paprika

Butter the bread and tear into small pieces. Layer the bread, bacon, sausage and cheese in a lightly buttered 3-quart baking dish. Whisk the eggs, milk, salt, dry mustard and paprika together in a mixing bowl. Pour over the layers in the baking dish. Bake at 350 degrees for 40 to 45 minutes or until puffed and a knife inserted near the center comes out clean.

Yield: 8 servings

TOBACCO ROAD TAILGATING

Tailgating pairs with the South like fried chicken and sweet tea! Each fall, students and alumni alike gather to cheer on their team. Whether it's the University of North Carolina Tar Heels or the Duke University Blue Devils, the atmosphere of camaraderie that comes from gathering together to enjoy good food and drink makes tailgating a favorite fall pastime.

Kale and Feta Quiche

Nonstick cooking spray or olive oil
1 cup chopped leeks
3 cups chopped kale
2 teaspoons minced fresh garlic
1 teaspoon dried herbs, such as rosemary, thyme, fennel, basil or a combination
Sea salt and freshly ground black pepper to taste
3 eggs plus 2 egg whites
2/3 cup almond milk
1/2 cup grated Gruyère cheese
1/4 teaspoon ground nutmeg
1/2 cup feta cheese
1 (9-inch) pie shell, baked

Coat a large skillet with nonstick cooking spray. Sauté the leeks, kale, garlic and herbs in the skillet over medium-high heat until wilted and all the liquid is evaporated. Season with salt and pepper. Let stand to cool. Whisk the eggs and egg whites, almond milk, Gruyère cheese and nutmeg in a mixing bowl. Season with salt and pepper. Spoon the leek mixture into the pie shell. Sprinkle with the feta cheese. Pour the egg mixture over the top, ensuring that the leek mixture and feta cheese are submerged to prevent burning. Bake at 400 degrees for about 25 minutes. Let stand to cool.

NOTE: To make a crustless version, omit the pie shell and spray the pie plate with nonstick cooking spray or coat with olive oil before adding the filling.

Yield: 8 servings

Brie and Mushroom Strata

1 large shallot, minced
2 tablespoons olive oil
2 cloves of garlic, minced
1 pound mixed mushrooms, such as
    bella, cremini or shiitake, sliced
Leaves of 3 or 4 sprigs of fresh thyme
1 tablespoon chopped fresh parsley
Pinch of salt
1/2 cup dry white wine
9 large eggs, lightly beaten

2 cups whole milk
1 cup heavy cream
2 tablespoons Dijon mustard
2 teaspoons kosher salt
Pinch of freshly ground black pepper
1 (8-ounce) round Brie cheese
1 (16-ounce) loaf day-old or toasted
    French bread, cut into 1/2-inch cubes
1/4 cup freshly grated Parmesan cheese

Sauté the shallot in the olive oil in a skillet over medium-high heat for 3 minutes or until tender. Add the garlic and sauté for 30 seconds. Add the mushrooms, thyme, parsley and pinch of salt. Sauté for 8 to 10 minutes or until the mushrooms are golden brown. Add the wine and increase the heat to high. Bring to a boil. Cook until the liquid is evaporated. Whisk the eggs, milk, cream, mustard, 2 teaspoons salt and pepper in a large mixing bowl.

Remove the rind from the Brie using a sharp knife and cut the cheese into 1/2-inch cubes. Layer half the bread, Brie, mushroom mixture and egg mixture in a buttered 7×11-inch baking dish. Repeat the layers and press gently to saturate the bread. Chill, covered with foil, for 2 hours to overnight. Place the covered baking dish on a baking sheet. Bake at 350 degrees for 1 hour. Remove the foil. Sprinkle with the Parmesan cheese. Bake, uncovered, for 15 to 25 minutes or until golden brown. Let stand until serving time.

Yield: 8 to 10 servings

Shrimp and Spinach Soufflé

5 1/3 tablespoons butter
1/3 cup all-purpose flour
1/2 teaspoon salt
1 3/4 cups milk
3/4 cup freshly grated Parmesan cheese

1/3 cup dry white wine
1 pound shrimp, cooked, peeled
  and chopped
1 1/2 cups cooked chopped spinach
8 eggs, separated

Melt the butter in a large saucepan. Stir in the flour to make a smooth paste. Add the salt and milk. Cook until thickened, stirring constantly; remove from the heat. Add the cheese and wine; mix well. Fold in the shrimp and spinach. Beat the egg yolks in a mixing bowl for 5 minutes or until thick. Stir into the shrimp mixture. Beat the egg whites using clean beaters until soft peaks form. Fold gently into the shrimp mixture until incorporated. Spoon into a soufflé dish. Place in a larger pan of hot water. Bake at 325 degrees for 1 hour or until set and browned on top.

Yield: 8 servings

Provençal Pie

1/3 cup breadcrumbs
3 or 4 medium tomatoes, sliced
1 medium onion, thinly sliced
1/2 cup grated mild Cheddar cheese
2 eggs
1/2 teaspoon salt

1/4 teaspoon dried oregano
Pepper to taste
1/3 cup breadcrumbs
1/4 cup freshly grated Parmesan cheese
3 slices bacon, partially cooked

Spread 1/3 cup breadcrumbs in a 9-inch pie plate. Layer with half the tomatoes, onion and Cheddar cheese. Layer with the remaining tomatoes, onion and Cheddar cheese. Beat the eggs in a small bowl. Add the salt, oregano and pepper and mix well. Pour over the layers. Sprinkle with a mixture of 1/3 cup breadcrumbs and Parmesan cheese. Top with the bacon. Bake at 350 degrees for 30 minutes.

Yield: 6 servings

Ricotta Crepes with Meaty Mushroom Sauce

MEATY MUSHROOM SAUCE

1 pound pork sausage
2 pounds ground round
4 large onions, chopped
1 cup minced fresh parsley
4 to 6 large cloves of garlic, minced
3/4 pound fresh mushrooms, thinly sliced
3 (15-ounce) cans of tomato sauce

1 fifth dry red table wine
2 teaspoons salt
1 teaspoon ground sage
1 teaspoon dried rosemary
1/2 teaspoon dried marjoram
1/2 teaspoon dried thyme
1/2 teaspoon freshly ground black pepper

RICOTTA CREPES

1 pound ricotta cheese
3/4 pound Monterey Jack cheese or
   domestic Muenster cheese, shredded
1/4 teaspoon nutmeg
1/8 teaspoon salt

Freshly ground black pepper to taste
12 prepared crepes
2 tablespoons butter
1 tablespoon freshly grated Parmesan
   cheese

For the Meaty Mushroom Sauce, brown the sausage and ground beef in a large Dutch oven over medium-low heat. Add the onions and sauté until tender. Add the parsley, garlic and mushrooms and stir to coat with the pan drippings. Stir in the tomato sauce, wine, salt, sage, rosemary, marjoram, thyme and pepper. Simmer, partially covered, for 3 hours or until the sauce is reduced and thickened, stirring occasionally. Skim off any excess fat.

For the Ricotta Crepes, combine the ricotta cheese, Monterey Jack cheese, nutmeg, salt and pepper in a bowl and mix well. Divide the mixture among the crepes, placing the mixture in the center of the crepe and folding up the sides. Arrange the crepes in a single layer in a buttered shallow baking dish. Dot the crepes with the butter and sprinkle with the Parmesan cheese. Bake at 350 degrees for 12 minutes or until bubbly. Top servings with the Meaty Mushroom Sauce.

NOTE: These crepes are delicious served with spinach salad and crusty bread. They can be assembled in the morning and cooked just before serving. The sauce freezes beautifully.

Yield: 6 servings

Roulade de Savoie

4 egg yolks
1/2 teaspoon salt
1/4 teaspoon freshly ground pepper
1/4 teaspoon ground nutmeg
2 tablespoons all-purpose flour
4 egg whites
1 tablespoon butter, softened
1 small zucchini, cut into julienne pieces
4 ounces mushrooms, thinly sliced

1 tablespoon butter
Salt and freshly ground pepper to taste
2 cups heavy cream
1 tablespoon butter, shaved
3/4 cup grated Gruyère cheese
2 ounces ham, cut into julienne pieces
3/4 cup grated Gruyère cheese
1/4 cup minced fresh parsley for garnish

Combine the egg yolks, 1/2 teaspoon salt, 1/4 teaspoon pepper and nutmeg in a mixing bowl. Beat for 10 minutes or until thick. Add the flour and mix well. Beat the egg whites in a mixing bowl using clean beaters until stiff peaks form. Fold into the egg yolk mixture. Line a jellyroll pan with waxed paper or parchment paper and spread with the softened butter. Spread the egg mixture 1/2 inch thick over the buttered paper. Bake at 350 degrees for 8 to 9 minutes. Turn out onto a clean sheet of waxed paper or parchment paper; peel off the first sheet. Sauté the zucchini and mushrooms in 1 tablespoon butter in a skillet for 2 to 3 minutes. Season with salt and pepper to taste.

Heat the cream and drizzle a generous amount over the egg layer, reserving the remaining cream. Dot with 1 tablespoon shaved butter. Sprinkle with 3/4 cup cheese, zucchini mixture and ham. Roll up from one long side as for a jellyroll. Place seam side down in a shallow baking dish. Pour the remaining cream around the roulade. May be set aside for up to 1 1/2 hours before baking. Sprinkle with 3/4 cup cheese. Bake at 375 degrees for 8 to 12 minutes or until golden brown. Garnish with the parsley. Cut into slices to serve.

Yield: 6 servings

Smoky Ham and Egg Cups

6 medium slices smoked deli ham
Nonstick cooking spray
6 large eggs
2 scallions, finely chopped
Salt and pepper to taste
1/2 to 3/4 cup baby spinach

Fit each ham slice into a muffin cup sprayed with nonstick cooking spray. Crack an egg into each ham cup. Sprinkle with scallions and season with salt and pepper. Arrange 3 or 4 spinach leaves on top of each. Bake at 400 degrees for 12 to 15 minutes or until the eggs are set and the ham is crisp. Serve warm.

VARIATIONS: Substitute 6 hollowed tomatoes or 6 seeded avocado halves for the ham.

Yield: 6 servings

Christmas Sausage Ring

2 pounds bulk mild sausage
2 eggs, lightly beaten
1/2 cup milk
2 cups breadcrumbs
1 small onion, diced
2 green apples, such as Granny Smith, diced

Combine the sausage, eggs, milk, breadcrumbs, onion and apples in a large bowl; mix well. Shape into a ring on a rimmed 9 x 12-inch nonstick baking pan. (The baking pan needs to have a high enough rim to hold the drippings.) Bake, loosely covered with foil, at 350 degrees for 1 hour. Remove the foil. Bake for 15 minutes longer or until browned.

Yield: 10 servings

BLOODY MARY

Stir 4 cups tomato juice, the juice of 2 limes, 2 tablespoons prepared horseradish, 1 tablespoon Worcestershire sauce and 1 teaspoon Tabasco sauce in a pitcher. Pour 1 ounce vodka over ice in each glass. Fill with the tomato juice mixture and stir. Garnish with a celery stalk, lime wedge, or olives.

Salmon Mousse

8 ounces smoked salmon
1 teaspoon unflavored gelatin
3 tablespoons cold water
1 1/4 cups sour cream
1 to 2 tablespoons fresh lemon juice

1/4 teaspoon kosher salt
Nonstick vegetable spray
1 teaspoon fresh dill weed
Nonstick vegetable spray

Divide the salmon into two 4-ounce portions. Refrigerate one portion. Soften the gelatin in the cold water in a saucepan for 5 minutes. Cook over low heat just until the gelatin is dissolved, stirring constantly; let stand to cool. Combine the remaining portion of the salmon, sour cream and lemon juice in a food processor and process until smooth. Add the salt. Add the cooled gelatin mixture gradually, processing constantly. Process until well mixed. Pour into a small springform pan sprayed with nonstick vegetable spray. Chill overnight. Unmold onto a serving plate. Cut the remaining portion of salmon into thin slices. Wrap the slices around the outside edge of the mousse. Serve with crackers or baguette slices.

Yield: 9 servings

Stuffed Artichoke Hearts

4 tablespoons butter, softened
1 clove of garlic, crushed
1 cup Parmesan cheese

1 can artichoke hearts,
    drained and cut into quarters
Paprika to taste

Beat the butter in a mixing bowl until creamy. Add the garlic and mix well. Stir in the cheese. Place the artichokes in a buttered baking dish. Spoon the cheese mixture on top of each. Sprinkle with paprika. Bake at 350 degrees until the cheese is browned.

Yield: 4 servings

Blueberry Chutney over Brie

from Cooking in Season with The Fresh Market

The Fresh Market celebrates great food! For more than 30 years, their commitment to freshness has been obvious in their name. Perishable goods will be sold only if the quality is high and the freshness is apparent. The Fresh Market stores provide a welcoming and relaxed destination to find the ingredients you need to make every meal special!

2 tablespoons sliced almonds
1 teaspoon vegetable oil
1 tablespoon minced shallot
1 small clove of garlic, minced
1/4 cup honey
2 teaspoons balsamic vinegar
1/2 teaspoon minced fresh rosemary

1/2 teaspoon dry mustard
1/8 teaspoon dried red pepper flakes
1 (6-ounce) package fresh blueberries
   (about 1 1/3 cups)
1 (12- to 14-ounce) wheel ripe Brie cheese,
   at room temperature
Minced fresh rosemary for garnish

Toast the almonds in a heated skillet over medium heat for about 2 minutes, stirring constantly. Transfer almonds to a small plate. Add the oil, shallot and garlic to the skillet. Sauté for about 2 minutes or until the shallot is tender. Add the honey, vinegar, 1/2 teaspoon rosemary, dry mustard and red pepper flakes. Bring to a simmer, stirring constantly. Add the blueberries. Cook for about 1 minute or just until warmed through; do not allow the blueberries to burst. Remove the top rind carefully from the Brie and place the Brie on a serving platter. Spoon the blueberry chutney over the top. Sprinkle with the toasted almonds and garnish with rosemary. Serve warm with crackers.

NOTE: This tasty appetizer, which balances the sweet flavor of blueberries with buttery Brie, will be ready in minutes, and it is likely to disappear from the table in record time, too. It works especially well with Brie, but try it over goat cheese or even a sharp Cheddar.

Yield: 4 to 6 servings

WINE SUGGESTION: Spanish or French rosé

Tomatoes Stuffed with Blue Cheese and Walnuts

4 medium tomatoes
Salt to taste
4 ounces blue cheese, crumbled
1/4 cup chopped walnuts

1/4 cup Italian-style breadcrumbs
1 tablespoon chopped fresh parsley
1/4 teaspoon pepper
1 tablespoon vegetable oil (optional)

Cut the tops off the tomatoes. Scoop out and discard the seeds. Season with salt. Spoon a mixture of the blue cheese, walnuts, breadcrumbs, parsley and pepper into each tomato cup, pressing the stuffing gently. Arrange on a baking sheet. Brush with the oil. Bake at 400 degrees for 10 to 15 minutes or until the tomatoes are tender and lightly browned.

NOTE: May use 2 large tomatoes, cut into halves, instead of 4 medium tomatoes.

Yield: 4 servings

Skinny Hash Brown Casserole

4 cups shredded potatoes
1 1/2 cups plain Greek yogurt
1/2 cup chicken broth
1/2 cup milk (at least 2-percent milk)
1 teaspoon garlic powder
1 teaspoon onion powder

1 teaspoon seasoned salt
1/2 teaspoon Italian seasoning
1/2 teaspoon freshly ground black pepper
Salt to taste
1 cup shredded Cheddar cheese
Nonstick cooking spray

Combine the potatoes, yogurt, broth, milk, garlic powder, onion powder, seasoned salt, Italian seasoning, pepper, salt and cheese in a large mixing bowl; stir until well mixed. Spread evenly in a baking dish sprayed with nonstick cooking spray. Bake at 350 degrees for 1 hour.

NOTE: This recipe is great to make the night before! Simply prepare the dish as directed; do not bake. Chill, covered, overnight and it will be ready to bake the following morning.

Yield: 6 to 8 servings

Sweet Potato Hash Browns

SAVORY HASH BROWNS

1 medium yellow onion, chopped
2 cloves of garlic, diced
1 teaspoon cayenne pepper
1 teaspoon Hungarian paprika

Salt and black pepper to taste
Olive oil
2 large sweet potatoes,
    cut into julienne pieces

SWEET HASH BROWNS

1 sweet onion, chopped
1 red, orange or yellow bell pepper,
    chopped (optional)
Ground nutmeg to taste
Ground cloves to taste

Allspice to taste
Butter
2 large sweet potatoes,
    cut into julienne pieces

For Savory Hash Browns, sauté the yellow onion, garlic, cayenne pepper, paprika, salt and pepper in a generous amount of olive oil in a medium skillet over medium heat until the onion is caramelized. Add the sweet potatoes. Cook over low heat until the sweet potatoes are tender and slightly blackened, stirring every 4 to 5 minutes. Season with additional salt and pepper.

For Sweet Hash Browns, sauté the sweet onion, bell pepper, nutmeg, cloves and allspice in a generous amount of butter in a medium skillet over medium heat until the onion is caramelized. Add the sweet potatoes. Cook over low heat until the sweet potatoes are tender and slightly blackened, stirring every 4 to 5 minutes.

NOTE: To perfectly julienne a sweet potato or other root vegetable, peel the potato first. If the bottom is round, cut a thin slice from the bottom so it will sit firmly and not roll on the cutting board. With flat side down, cut into 1/8-inch slices. Stack the slices, then cut into 1/8-inch strips. The strips can then be cut into whatever length is desired.

Yield: 4 to 6 servings

Peppery White Cheddar Biscuits

4 cups all-purpose flour
2 tablespoons baking powder
1/2 teaspoon salt
1/2 cup shortening
4 tablespoons butter

1 1/2 cups shredded white sharp Cheddar cheese
2 to 3 teaspoons coarsely ground pepper
1 1/2 cups milk
1 egg, beaten
1/2 teaspoon water

Combine the flour, baking powder and salt in a large bowl. Cut in the shortening and butter using a pastry blender until the mixture resembles coarse crumbs. Add the cheese and pepper and mix well. Make a well in the center of the cheese mixture. Pour the milk into the well and stir just until the flour mixture is moistened.

Turn the dough out onto a lightly floured surface. Knead gently to incorporate any surface flour. Divide the dough into halves. Roll or pat each half into a 6-inch square, about 1-inch thick. Cut the dough into 2-inch squares using a long sharp knife. Arrange the biscuits on a large greased baking sheet so they are almost touching. Mix the egg and water in a bowl. Brush over the biscuits.

Bake at 400 degrees for 12 to 14 minutes or until lightly browned. Remove from the baking sheet and serve piping hot.

Yield: 18 biscuits

Strawberry Bruschetta

1 French baguette, cut into 16 slices
1 pint strawberries, rinsed and sliced
Zest and juice of 1 orange

1/2 teaspoon vanilla extract
2 tablespoons sugar

Arrange the baguette slices on a baking sheet. Toast at 350 degrees for 10 minutes or until light golden brown. Combine the strawberries, orange zest, orange juice, vanilla and 1 tablespoon of the sugar in a bowl and mix well. Spoon over the warm baguette slices. Sprinkle with the remaining 1 tablespoon sugar. Caramelize the sugar using a torch, or place under a broiler set at high for 2 minutes, watching carefully.

Yield: 16 servings

Sour Cream Corn Bread

1 cup self-rising cornmeal
1 teaspoon baking powder
1 teaspoon sugar
2 eggs, beaten
1 (8-ounce) container sour cream
1 (8-ounce) can cream-style corn
1/2 cup vegetable oil

Combine the cornmeal, baking powder and sugar in a mixing bowl; mix well. Add a mixture of the eggs, sour cream, corn and oil; mix well. Pour into a greased square baking pan. Bake at 375 degrees for 35 to 40 minutes or until golden brown.

Yield: 9 servings

Mexican Corn Bread

1 1/2 cups self-rising yellow cornmeal
2 eggs
1 cup buttermilk
1/2 cup vegetable oil
1 (8-ounce) can whole kernel corn, drained
1 cup freshly grated extra-sharp Cheddar cheese
1 cup chopped onion
Diced jalapeño peppers (optional)
Nonstick cooking spray

Combine the cornmeal, eggs, buttermilk, oil, corn, cheese and onion in a large mixing bowl. Stir with a fork until well mixed. Spoon into muffin cups sprayed with nonstick cooking spray. Sprinkle with jalapeños for an extra kick. Bake at 350 degrees for 25 minutes or until a wooden pick inserted in the centers comes out clean.

Yield: 12 muffins

Buttermilk Hush Puppies with Heirloom Tomato Jam

HEIRLOOM TOMATO JAM

4 ounces bacon, diced
1/4 cup local honey
1/4 cup agave nectar
1/4 cup sugar
1/2 cup apple cider vinegar
2 cloves of garlic, pulverized
1 tablespoon grated fresh ginger

1 1/2 teaspoons ground cumin
1 teaspoon ground cinnamon
1/4 teaspoon ground nutmeg
1/4 teaspoon cayenne pepper
2 pounds heirloom tomatoes, finely diced
3/4 teaspoon salt
1/4 teaspoon pepper

BUTTERMILK HUSH PUPPIES

1 cup cornmeal
1 cup all-purpose flour
3 tablespoons packed brown sugar
1 tablespoon baking powder
1/4 teaspoon kosher salt
1 cup plus 2 tablespoons cold buttermilk

1 egg, beaten
1 tablespoon butter, melted
2 tablespoons bacon drippings (reserved
    from Heirloom Tomato Jam recipe)
Vegetable oil for deep-frying
1/4 teaspoon kosher salt

For the Heirloom Tomato Jam, cook the bacon in a skillet until crispy; remove to a plate. Reserve 2 tablespoons of the bacon drippings for the hush puppy recipe. Melt the honey and agave nectar in a medium saucepan over medium heat, stirring constantly. Add the sugar and cook until dissolved, stirring constantly. Stir in the vinegar, garlic, ginger, cumin, cinnamon, nutmeg and cayenne pepper. Add the tomatoes and mix well. Bring the mixture to a boil. Cook for 5 minutes, stirring occasionally. Reduce the heat and simmer for 45 minutes. Season with the salt and pepper. Let stand to cool. Chill until the jam is thickened to the desired consistency.

For the Buttermilk Hush Puppies, combine the cornmeal, flour, brown sugar, baking powder and 1/4 teaspoon salt in a large metal bowl. Combine the buttermilk, egg, butter and bacon drippings in a small bowl and mix well. Add the buttermilk mixture to the cornmeal mixture gradually, folding until the batter is smooth after each addition. Heat 3 inches of oil in a Dutch oven to 350 degrees on a candy thermometer. Drop the batter by teaspoonfuls into the oil. Deep-fry for about 4 minutes or until golden brown. Drain on a wire rack. Season with 1/4 teaspoon salt. Place on a baking sheet. Keep warm in a 200-degree oven until serving time. Serve with the Heirloom Tomato Jam.

Yield: 3 dozen hush puppies

Sour Cream Pecan Coffee Cake

Bubba Cunningham has been the athletic director at the University of North Carolina at Chapel Hill since 2011. On game days, this coffee cake often serves as the perfect precursor to a day full of Tar Heel athletics for Bubba, his wife, Tina, and their guests.

1 cup butter, softened
2 cups sugar
2 egg yolks
2 cups all-purpose flour, sifted
1 teaspoon baking powder
1/4 teaspoon salt
1 teaspoon vanilla extract

1 cup sour cream
2 egg whites, stiffly beaten
1/2 cup chopped pecans
1/4 cup packed brown sugar
1 teaspoon cinnamon
Confectioners' sugar to taste

Beat the butter and sugar in a mixing bowl until light and fluffy. Add the egg yolks and beat until light. Add a mixture of the flour, baking powder and salt; mix well. Fold in the vanilla, sour cream and egg whites gently. Spoon half the batter into a greased and floured Bundt pan. Sprinkle a mixture of the pecans, brown sugar and cinnamon over the batter. Top with the remaining batter. Bake at 350 degrees for 50 to 60 minutes or until the coffee cake tests done; do not overbake. Let cool in the pan on a wire rack. Loosen the edges with a knife and invert onto a serving plate. Sprinkle with confectioners' sugar.

NOTE: This coffee cake keeps well when wrapped in plastic wrap.

Yield: 12 servings

Chocolate and Nut Banana Bread

1/2 cup shortening
1 cup sugar
2 eggs
3 overripe bananas, mashed
2 cups all-purpose flour

1/4 teaspoon salt
1 teaspoon baking soda
1/4 cup nuts
1/4 cup chocolate chips

Cream the shortening, sugar and eggs in a mixing bowl. Add the bananas and mix well. Mix the flour, salt and baking soda together. Add to the banana mixture. Stir in the chocolate chips and nuts.

Pour into a greased and floured 5×9-inch loaf pan. Bake at 350 degrees for 1 hour or until a wooden pick inserted in the center comes out clean.

Yield: 9 servings

Bananas Foster Bread

1 1/2 cups mashed ripe bananas
1/2 cup packed brown sugar
5 tablespoons butter
3 tablespoons Cognac, dark rum or milk
1/3 cup fat-free Greek yogurt
2 large eggs
1/2 cup packed brown sugar
3/4 cup all-purpose flour

3/4 cup whole wheat flour
3/4 teaspoon baking soda
1/2 teaspoon salt
1/2 teaspoon ground cinnamon
1/8 teaspoon allspice
1 tablespoon butter
1 tablespoon Cognac, dark rum or milk
1/3 cup confectioners' sugar

Combine the bananas, 1/2 cup brown sugar, 5 tablespoons butter and 3 tablespoons Cognac in a nonstick skillet. Cook until the mixture begins to bubble, stirring frequently; remove from the heat. Let stand to cool. Spoon the mixture into a large mixing bowl. Add the yogurt, eggs and 1/2 cup brown sugar. Beat at medium speed until fluffy. Add a mixture of the all-purpose flour, whole wheat flour, baking soda, salt, cinnamon and allspice gradually, beating until blended. Pour into a 5×9-inch loaf pan sprayed with nonstick cooking spray. Bake at 350 degrees for 1 hour or until the bread tests done. Cool on a wire rack for 10 minutes. Remove the bread to a wire rack. Combine 1 tablespoon butter, 1 tablespoon Cognac and the confectioners' sugar in a bowl; stir until blended. Drizzle over the warm bread.

Yield: 12 servings

Heart-Healthy Pumpkin Bread

1 (15-ounce) can pumpkin purée
1/2 cup egg whites
2/3 cup vegetable oil
1/4 cup plus 3 tablespoons water
1 cup packed brown sugar
1 cup sugar
1 1/3 cups all-purpose flour
1 cup whole wheat flour

1 1/4 teaspoons baking soda
1 teaspoon salt
3/4 teaspoon ground nutmeg
1/4 teaspoon ground cloves
1/8 teaspoon ground ginger
1/8 teaspoon pumpkin pie spice
Nonstick cooking spray
2 tablespoons pepitas (pumpkin seeds)

Combine the pumpkin puree, egg whites, oil, water, brown sugar and sugar in a large mixing bowl; beat until blended. Whisk the all-purpose flour, whole wheat flour, baking soda, salt, nutmeg, cloves, ginger and pumpkin pie spice in a bowl. Stir into the pumpkin mixture until well blended. Spoon half the batter into each of two 3 x 7-inch loaf pans sprayed with nonstick cooking spray. Sprinkle with the pepitas. Bake at 350 degrees for 45 to 50 minutes or until the bread tests done. Cool on wire racks for 10 to 15 minutes before serving.

Yield: 18 servings

Mini Monkey Bread Muffins

12 Sister Shubert frozen dinner rolls,
   partially thawed
6 tablespoons butter, melted
2 tablespoons light corn syrup
1/2 cup packed light brown sugar

2 teaspoons cinnamon
1 cup confectioners' sugar
1 tablespoon butter, melted
1 to 2 tablespoons milk
1/2 teaspoon vanilla extract

Grease 12 muffin cup liners and place in muffin cups. Cut each dinner roll into 4 portions. Combine 6 tablespoons butter and corn syrup in a small bowl; mix well. Mix the brown sugar and cinnamon in a small bowl. Dip each roll portion into the butter and coat with the brown sugar mixture. Place 4 roll portions in each prepared muffin cup. Cover the rolls with plastic wrap. Let stand for 15 minutes; remove the plastic wrap. Bake at 350 degrees for 15 to 20 minutes or until puffed and brown. Whisk the confectioners' sugar, 1 tablespoon butter, milk and vanilla in a small bowl until smooth. Drizzle over the hot muffins.

Yield: 12 muffins

Sweet Potato Muffins

4 medium or large sweet potatoes
1 cup milk
4 tablespoons butter, melted
1 cup sugar
2 eggs
1 (5-ounce) cup Greek-style vanilla yogurt
1 teaspoon vanilla extract
2 teaspoons ground cinnamon
1 teaspoon ground nutmeg
2 cups all-purpose flour
3/4 teaspoon baking soda
1 teaspoon salt
Nonstick cooking spray

Bake the sweet potatoes at 400 degrees for 1 hour or until tender; cool. Remove the pulp from the skins and place in a large bowl. Mash with a potato masher or fork until smooth. Whisk in the milk, butter, sugar, eggs, yogurt, vanilla, cinnamon and nutmeg. Mix the flour, baking soda and salt in a small bowl. Add the flour mixture to the sweet potato mixture gradually, mixing well after each addition. Spoon 1/4 cup of the batter into each of 12 muffin cups sprayed with nonstick cooking spray. Bake at 350 degrees for 50 minutes or until the muffins test done.

Yield: 12 muffins

CAROLINA SWEET POTATOES

The sweet potato, a crop native to North Carolina, has been the state's official vegetable since 1995, and we have been the top sweet potato–producer in the United States since 1971. North Carolina sweet potatoes are available all year long. When selecting sweet potatoes, it is important that they are firm to the touch. Choose sweet potatoes that are uniform in shape and size for even cooking. Sweet potatoes can be stored in a cool, dry, and well-ventilated container for up to two weeks.

Taste the Freshness
SOUPS AND SALADS

Farms and Families of Tobacco Road

The heart and soul of Tobacco Road is found in the stories and histories of the families who call this area home. From wheat and corn to cotton and tobacco, thriving plantations put this area on the map, and several of these homes are well preserved to this day.

Hardscrabble Plantation was home to the family of William Cain. By 1800, he was the largest land owner in Orange County, with over 4,400 acres in his name. Four generations of the Cain family called Hardscrabble home, and it continued to be a working plantation until 1878, when the land started to be sold gradually. The house is a private residence today with much of the land developed into a neighborhood.

With the union of the Cameron and Bennehan families in 1803, Stagville Plantation and its surrounding 30,000 acres became one of the largest plantation complexes in the South. Nearby Horton Grove is an area of two-story slave residences built in 1850. These residences are well preserved and have given historians a glimpse into the lives of the slaves who lived and worked at Stagville. Liggett and Myers Tobacco Company bought and farmed the land, donating some acreage to the state of North Carolina. Stagville, a historic house museum, is open to the public.

Although this area was home to many crops, tobacco was king, and few families were as successful in this industry as the family of Washington Duke. Following the end of the Civil War, Duke started farming and manufacturing tobacco on a small farm north of Durham. By 1880, his son James B. Duke expanded the company into a mass manufacturing and marketing firm and eventually became the president of the American Tobacco Company. The Duke Homestead, a state historic site, is open to the public as an example of a nineteenth century family farm and small-scale tobacco factory. The Duke family left its philanthropic stamp all over Durham, establishing Duke University (formerly Trinity College) through a generous endowment of $19 million in 1924. The following year, an additional bequest helped establish a medical school, hospital, and school of nursing. Today, Duke University Medical Center is one of the top medical treatment centers and schools in the world.

Chilled Blackberry Soup with Stewed Peaches and Candied Almonds

CANDIED ALMONDS

1 cup sliced almonds
1 egg white

1/4 cup sugar
Dash of cinnamon

STEWED PEACHES

4 fresh peaches, peeled
3/4 cup tawny port
1/2 cup sugar

1/3 teaspoon ground nutmeg
1 cinnamon stick
1/2 teaspoon vanilla extract

SOUP

6 cups blackberries
1 cup peach juice or other fruit juice
3/4 cup honey
1/3 cup water
1 tablespoon lemon juice

1/4 teaspoon ground cinnamon
1/4 teaspoon ground nutmeg
1 1/2 cups plain yogurt
1/4 teaspoon vanilla extract

For the Candied Almonds, spread the almonds on a baking sheet. Bake at 350 degrees for 10 minutes or until fragrant; do not burn. Increase the oven temperature to 375 degrees. Beat the egg white in a mixing bowl until soft peaks form. Fold in the sugar, cinnamon and almonds. Spread as thinly as possible on a parchment-lined baking sheet. Bake for 10 minutes or until very lightly browned, turning once. Let stand to cool. Break up any large clusters.

For the Stewed Peaches, cut each peach into 8 slices, discarding the pits. Combine the port, sugar, nutmeg, cinnamon stick and vanilla in a large saucepan over medium-high heat. Bring to a boil; reduce the heat to medium. Add the peaches and stir to coat. Cook for about 10 minutes or until the peaches are tender, stirring occasionally. Discard the cinnamon stick. Let stand to cool.

For the Soup, combine the blackberries, peach juice, honey, water, lemon juice, cinnamon and nutmeg in a large saucepan. Bring to a boil; reduce the heat to low. Simmer for about 25 minutes or until the blackberries are tender and breaking apart, stirring occasionally. Remove from the heat; cool slightly. Stir in the yogurt and vanilla. Purée in batches until thoroughly blended. Chill, covered, for 3 hours to overnight. Ladle into soup bowls. Spoon several slices of the Stewed Peaches and 2 tablespoons of the peach syrup onto each serving and top with 1 to 2 tablespoons of the Candied Almonds.

Yield: 4 to 6 servings

Chilled Cucumber Soup

2 cucumbers, peeled and seeded
1 1/2 cups chicken broth
1 1/2 cups sour cream
2 teaspoons (or more) rice vinegar
1 teaspoon salt, or to taste

White pepper to taste
Chopped green onions to taste
Chopped cucumbers, chopped tomatoes
   and pumpkin seeds for garnish

Combine the seeded cucumbers, broth, sour cream, vinegar, salt, white pepper and green onions in a blender or food processor. Process until blended and smooth. Chill, covered, in the refrigerator. Pour into soup bowls. Garnish or serve with chopped cucumbers, tomatoes and pumpkin seeds.

NOTE: May use fat-free sour cream.

Yield: 4 servings

Black Bean Soup

1 small onion, chopped
3 cloves of garlic, minced
1/4 teaspoon cayenne pepper
2 tablespoons olive oil
1 teaspoon ground cumin
2 cups homemade chicken stock

3 (15-ounce) cans stewed tomatoes
3 (16-ounce) cans black beans, rinsed and
   drained
1/4 cup chopped cilantro
Plain Greek yogurt or crème fraîche for garnish

Sauté the onion, garlic and cayenne pepper in the olive oil in a large saucepan for about 5 minutes or until the onion is translucent. Add the cumin, stock and tomatoes, stirring to break up the tomatoes. Cover and bring to a boil. Add the beans and cilantro. Blend to desired consistency using an immersion blender. Serve warm. Garnish with yogurt or crème fraîche.

Yield: 6 to 8 servings

Pasta and Bean Soup

1/2 onion, diced
3 cloves of garlic, minced
1 tablespoon olive oil
2 (15-ounce) cans Great Northern beans
15 ounces water
32 ounces (4 cups) fat-free chicken or vegetable broth
1 (15-ounce) can diced tomatoes
1 rib of celery, chopped
3 carrots, chopped
1 tablespoon dried basil
1 tablespoon dried parsley
1 teaspoon dried oregano
2 bay leaves
Salt and pepper to taste
1 cup water
6 ounces small pasta shells
Freshly grated Parmesan cheese to taste

Sauté the onion and garlic in the olive oil in a stockpot over medium heat until the onion is translucent. Combine 1 can of the beans and 15 ounces water in a blender and process until smooth. Add to the stockpot with the whole beans, broth, tomatoes, celery, carrots, basil, parsley, oregano, bay leaves, salt and pepper. Stir in 1 cup water. Bring to a boil; reduce the heat. Simmer for 20 to 30 minutes, stirring occasionally. Remove the bay leaves. Add the pasta shells. Cook, uncovered, until the pasta is tender. Ladle into soup bowls. Top with Parmesan cheese.

Yield: 8 servings

Easy Beef and Barley Soup

1/4 cup dried wild mushrooms
1/2 cup water
1 pound beef stew meat, cut into 1/2-inch cubes
Salt and pepper to taste
2 tablespoons olive oil
1 medium onion, finely chopped
2 carrots, peeled and finely chopped
1 teaspoon dried thyme
4 cups beef broth
2/3 cup quick-cooking barley

Combine the mushrooms and water in a microwave-safe bowl and cover with a paper towel. Microwave on High for 1 minute. Let stand for several minutes. Drain the mushrooms, reserving the liquid. Chop the mushrooms finely. Season the beef with salt and pepper and brown in 1 tablespoon olive oil in a soup pot or Dutch oven over medium-high heat. Transfer to a plate and cover to keep warm. Add the remaining 1 tablespoon olive oil to the pan drippings. Sauté the onion, carrots and thyme in the soup pot for 5 to 10 minutes or until the carrots are tender. Add the broth, reserved mushroom liquid, beef and barley. Bring to a boil; reduce the heat. Simmer, covered, for 10 to 15 minutes or until the barley is tender, stirring occasionally.

Yield: 4 to 6 servings

Goulash Soup

1 pound lean ground beef or ground turkey
1 onion, diced
2 ribs of celery, diced
2 carrots, diced
1 package Lipton onion soup mix
1 teaspoon minced garlic
$1/2$ teaspoon dried thyme
$1/2$ teaspoon pepper
$1/2$ teaspoon red pepper flakes

1 teaspoon Italian seasoning
16 ounces fat-free beef broth
1 (15-ounce) can petite diced tomatoes
1 cup water
8 ounces green peas
1 pound russet potatoes, peeled, cubed
$1/3$ cup sour cream
2 tablespoons butter, diced
$1/4$ teaspoon salt

Cook the ground beef in a large skillet over medium-high heat just until browned, stirring occasionally; drain. Combine the ground beef, onion, celery and carrots in a soup pot. Cook for 10 minutes, stirring occasionally. Add the soup mix, garlic, thyme, pepper, red pepper flakes and Italian seasoning; mix well. Add the broth, tomatoes and water. Simmer just until the vegetables are tender, stirring occasionally. Reserve 8 to 12 peas for garnish. Add the remaining peas to the soup pot. Place the potatoes in a large saucepan with water to cover. Bring to a boil; reduce the heat. Simmer, covered, for 15 to 20 minutes or until tender; drain. Return the potatoes to the saucepan. Add the sour cream, butter and salt. Mash until smooth. Ladle the soup into soup bowls. Top with the mashed potatoes.

Yield: 4 to 6 servings

Chicken, Cauliflower and Leek Soup

3 large leeks
1 (32-ounce) carton vegetable broth
1 (32-ounce) carton chicken broth
8 ounces cream cheese

2 1/2 cups chopped cooked chicken, or
  2 (12-ounce) cans chicken, drained
1 head cauliflower, chopped

Wash the leeks thoroughly to remove any sand particles. Trim and discard the green leaves. Chop the leeks. Combine the vegetable broth, chicken broth and cream cheese in a soup pot. Heat over medium heat until the cream cheese begins to melt. Add the leeks and bring to a boil. Reduce the heat to medium-low. Simmer, covered, for 10 minutes. Stir in the chicken and cauliflower. Cook over medium heat for 5 to 10 minutes or until the vegetables are tender.

Yield: 8 servings

Slow Cooker Taco Soup

1 1/4 pounds boneless skinless chicken
  breasts
1 tablespoon vegetable oil
1 (12-ounce) jar roasted garlic salsa
1 (14-ounce) can diced tomatoes
2 cups low-sodium chicken broth
1 (16-ounce) package frozen corn, thawed

1 large white onion, chopped
1/2 jalapeño pepper, minced
2 chipotle chilies in adobo sauce
3 corn tortillas, chopped
Chopped fresh cilantro, diced avocado, low-fat
  Greek yogurt, shredded Monterey Jack cheese
  and tortilla chips for garnish

Cook the chicken in the oil in a skillet over high heat for 3 to 5 minutes per side or until cooked through. Place in a slow cooker. Add the salsa, tomatoes, broth, corn, onion, jalapeño pepper, chipotle chilies and corn tortillas. Cook on Low for 7 to 9 hours. Remove the chicken carefully and shred using 2 forks. Return the chicken to the soup and stir to incorporate. Ladle into soup bowls. Garnish with cilantro, avocado, yogurt, cheese and tortilla chips.

Yield: 6 to 8 servings

Shrimp and Corn Soup

1 cup lightly browned roux (see sidebar)
1 1/2 medium onions, chopped
2 large cloves of garlic, minced
4 tablespoons unsalted butter
2 to 3 tablespoons extra-virgin olive oil
8 cups seafood stock
8 cups fresh yellow corn
2 cups heavy cream
2 to 3 pounds fresh jumbo shrimp,
    peeled and deveined
Sea salt, freshly ground black pepper, cayenne
    pepper and Mrs. Dash Table Blends to taste
2 cups cooked brown rice (optional)

Heat the roux in an iron skillet, adding no oil to the skillet. Sauté the onions and garlic in the butter and olive oil in a stockpot until the onions are translucent. Whisk in the roux. Add the stock gradually and stir until blended. Add the corn. Bring to a rolling boil; reduce the heat. Stir in the cream. Cook at a high simmer for 1 to 1 1/2 hours, stirring frequently to prevent the mixture from sticking to the bottom. Add the shrimp. Cook for 20 minutes. Season with sea salt, black pepper, cayenne pepper and Mrs. Dash. Serve over the brown rice.

Yield: 8 to 10 servings

ROUX

A roux is a mixture of fat and flour used to thicken sauces. It can be made with a variety of oils and fats. For a basic roux, melt 1 cup butter in a saucepan over medium heat until the foam subsides. Whisk in 3/4 cup all-purpose or gluten-free flour; do not use whole wheat flour. Cook until a thick paste forms, whisking constantly. The mixture will be bubbly. Cook until the roux is the desired color and texture. Remove from the heat.

Washington Duke's Shrimp, Corn and Bacon Chowder

THE WASHINGTON DUKE INN

The Washington Duke Inn is a prestigious hotel near Duke University. The inn first opened its doors in 1988 to serve the needs of Durham's growing business community. The hotel is named for Washington Duke (1820–1905). From his modest beginnings as an American Civil War soldier with a mule and fifty cents to his name, he went on to become a philanthropist and industrialist. His tobacco farm eventually grew to become the American Tobacco Company.

1/2 cup chopped thickly sliced bacon
1/2 cup unsalted butter
1 pound carrots, diced
1 pound onions, diced
1 pound celery, diced
1/2 cup all-purpose flour
1 tablespoon dried thyme
1 tablespoon dried basil
Salt and pepper to taste
51/2 cups clam juice
11/2 cups corn
1 pound Idaho potatoes, diced
6 cups heavy cream
3/4 pound fresh shrimp, peeled and deveined

Cook the bacon in a heavy stockpot over medium heat until crisp; drain. Add the butter, carrots, onions and celery and sauté until tender. Add the flour, thyme, basil, salt and pepper. Cook for about 5 minutes, stirring constantly. Add the clam juice gradually, whisking until the mixture is smooth. Bring to a simmer. Add the corn and potatoes. Simmer for 10 minutes. Add the cream. Return to a simmer, stirring frequently. Add the shrimp. Season to taste and remove from the heat. Let stand for 5 minutes or until the shrimp are cooked through.

Yield: 10 to 12 servings

Butternut Squash Soup with Sage Croutons

SAGE CROUTONS
4 slices day-old firmly textured white bread
3 tablespoons olive oil
4 fresh sage leaves

BUTTERNUT SQUASH SOUP
1 small butternut squash, peeled, seeded and cut into cubes
1 sweet potato, peeled and sliced
1 small onion, chopped
5 cups chicken stock
Salt and pepper to taste
Crème fraîche for garnish

For the Sage Croutons, remove the crusts from the bread and cut the bread into small cubes. Heat the olive oil and sage in a skillet. Sauté the bread in the hot oil until golden brown. Remove to paper towels to drain.

For the Butternut Squash Soup, combine the squash, sweet potato, onion and stock in a large saucepan. Bring to a boil; reduce the heat. Simmer for about 30 minutes or until the vegetables are tender. Purée the vegetables using an immersion blender. Season with salt and pepper. Serve warm topped with the Sage Croutons and garnished with crème fraîche.

Yield: 6 servings

Vegan Butternut Squash Soup

1/2 medium yellow onion, diced
Vegetable oil or water
1 (1-inch) piece fresh ginger, minced
3 medium cloves of garlic, minced
1/2 teaspoon ground nutmeg
1 large butternut squash, peeled, seeded and cut into cubes (about 2 cups)
2 medium yellow potatoes, peeled and cut into cubes
Sea salt and pepper to taste

Sauté the onion in a small amount of oil or water in a medium saucepan until translucent. Add the ginger, garlic and nutmeg. Sauté for a few minutes longer. Add the squash, potatoes and enough water to cover the vegetables. Cover and bring to a boil; reduce the heat. Simmer for 30 minutes or until the squash and potatoes are tender. Purée using an immersion blender until smooth. Season with salt and pepper. Serve hot.

Yield: 4 servings

VEGAN VS. VEGETARIAN

If you're a meat eater, you may wonder what the true difference is between being a vegan and being a vegetarian. Although similar in many ways, the two differ dramatically. Vegetarians tend to consume dairy products and eggs, while vegans avoid all animal products, including eggs, dairy, and, in some cases, even animal-based products such as leather or fur. While both abstain from eating meat, vegetarianism is viewed as a diet while being a vegan is a lifestyle choice.

Creamy Tomato Soup

1 medium onion, finely chopped
1 medium carrot, finely chopped
1 rib of celery, finely chopped
2 cloves of garlic, finely chopped
2 tablespoons unsalted butter
3 tablespoons flour
4 cups chicken stock
1 (14-ounce) can diced tomatoes, drained
1 (14-ounce) can fire-roasted tomatoes, drained
3 tablespoons tomato paste
2 teaspoons sugar
1 1/4 cups heavy cream
2 tablespoons unsalted butter
Salt and pepper to taste

Sauté the onion, carrot, celery and garlic in 2 tablespoons butter in a large saucepan for about 5 minutes; do not let the garlic brown. Sprinkle with the flour. Cook for 1 minute longer, stirring constantly. Stir in the stock, diced tomatoes, fire-roasted tomatoes, tomato paste and sugar. Bring to a boil. Cook, partially covered, for 15 minutes, stirring occasionally. Process in a blender or using an immersion blender for about 20 to 30 seconds or until partially puréed. Stir in the cream and 2 tablespoons butter. Season with salt and pepper.

NOTE: You may substitute 2 cans fire-roasted tomatoes or 2 cans diced tomatoes for the diced and fire-roasted tomatoes.

Yield: 6 to 8 servings

CHICKEN STOCK

Making your own chicken stock is easy and will provide a richer, more complex flavor than using store-bought stock. Combine 1 whole chicken, 1 quartered onion, 4 peeled and chopped carrots, 4 chopped ribs of celery, fresh thyme and parsley to taste, 2 bay leaves, 8 to 10 peppercorns, and 2 cloves of garlic in a large stockpot or slow cooker. Add enough water to cover. Bring almost to the boiling point over high heat; reduce the heat. Simmer for 6 to 8 hours. Strain and chill the stock overnight.

Vegetarian Chili

1 green bell pepper, chopped
1 red bell pepper, chopped
1 onion, chopped
Vegetable oil or water
2 1/2 tablespoons chili powder
1 tablespoon ground cumin
2 teaspoons dried thyme
2 (14-ounce) cans peeled diced tomatoes
1 (10-ounce) can tomatoes with green chilies
1 (15-ounce) can corn, drained
2 (15-ounce) cans black beans, partially drained
1 (15-ounce) can dark red kidney beans, partially drained
Juice of 1/2 lemon
Salt and pepper to taste

Sauté the green bell pepper, red bell pepper and onion in a small amount of oil or water until tender-crisp. Add the chili powder, cumin and thyme. Cook for several minutes, stirring constantly. Combine the undrained tomatoes, undrained tomatoes with green chilies, corn, black beans and kidney beans in a large stockpot or slow cooker. Add the sautéed vegetables. Stir in the lemon juice. Season with salt and pepper. Cook over low heat for several hours, stirring occasionally.

NOTE: The longer it cooks, the better it will be.

Yield: 6 servings

Carolina Brunswick Stew

With multiple locations claiming to be the birthplace of this traditional Southern stew, all we know is that it's been a Carolina favorite for generations. No pig-pickin' or lowcountry boil is complete without it! Throw in the Buttermilk Hush Puppies on page 56 for a true Tobacco Road experience.

2 (2 1/2-pound) chickens
Carrots to taste
Celery to taste
5 medium onions, sliced
1 (28-ounce) can whole tomatoes
1 (14-ounce) can whole tomatoes
1 (6-ounce) can tomato paste
1/2 teaspoon sugar
2 (15-ounce) cans cream-style corn
2 (15-ounce) cans lima beans, drained
1/4 cup Worcestershire sauce
2 tablespoons unsalted butter
2 bay leaves

Place the chickens, carrots and celery in a Dutch oven with enough water to cover. Bring to a boil. Reduce the heat to low. Simmer until the chicken is cooked through. Remove the chicken from the broth, reserving the broth. Let the chicken stand to cool. Shred the chicken, discarding the skin and bones. (Chicken may be cooked up to 1 day in advance.)

Combine the shredded chicken, 1 cup of the reserved broth, onions, tomatoes, tomato paste and sugar in a Dutch oven. Cook over medium-low heat for 2 hours, stirring occasionally. Add the corn, lima beans, Worcestershire sauce, butter and bay leaves. Simmer for 30 minutes, stirring occasionally. Remove and discard the bay leaves. Serve hot.

NOTE: May refrigerate, covered, for up to 1 day. Reheat when ready to serve. The stew may also be frozen.

Yield: 10 to 12 servings

Summer Beet Salad

2 bunches of beets
1 to 1 1/2 cups blueberries
8 to 10 mint leaves, torn into
   small pieces

1 to 2 tablespoons honey
1 tablespoon olive oil
1 teaspoon fresh lemon juice
2 ounces chèvre cheese or feta cheese

Trim the leaves from the beets and wrap the beets in foil. Roast at 400 degrees for 45 to 60 minutes or until the largest beet can be pierced easily with a fork. Cool completely. Peel the beets and cut into 1/4-inch slices. Arrange the beets, blueberries and mint on a plate. Drizzle with a mixture of the honey, olive oil and lemon juice. Sprinkle with the cheese.

NOTE: Any color of beets will work for this recipe, but golden beets or candy-striped beets make a pretty presentation.

Yield: 6 to 8 servings

Fresh Broccoli and Raisin Salad

5 bunches of broccoli
8 ounces bacon, crisp-fried and crumbled
1 red onion, chopped or finely slivered
1 cup raisins

1/2 cup sunflower seeds
1 cup mayonnaise
1/4 cup sugar
2 tablespoons white vinegar

Break the broccoli into small florets, discarding the large stems. Combine the broccoli, bacon, onion, raisins and sunflower seeds in a large bowl. Combine the mayonnaise, sugar and vinegar in a small bowl and mix well. Add to the broccoli mixture and toss to coat. Cover and chill thoroughly before serving.

Yield: 6 servings

Avocado and Tomato Stacks

2 to 4 slices bacon, cut into halves
1 1/4 cups buttermilk
1 tablespoon finely chopped fresh chives
1 tablespoon finely chopped fresh basil
2 tablespoons mayonnaise
2 teaspoons apple cider vinegar
1 clove of garlic, minced
1/4 teaspoon freshly ground black pepper
2 ears of corn, shucked (optional)
Nonstick cooking spray
2 large beefsteak tomatoes
2 globe tomatoes
1/2 teaspoon kosher salt
1 avocado, peeled and thinly sliced
4 teaspoons extra-virgin olive oil
1/4 teaspoon freshly ground black pepper

Cook the bacon in a large nonstick skillet over medium heat for 8 minutes or until crisp, tossing occasionally to curl the bacon; drain on paper towels. Combine the buttermilk, chives, basil, mayonnaise, vinegar and garlic in a small bowl; whisk to blend. Stir in 1/4 teaspoon pepper. Coat the corn with nonstick cooking spray. Place on the rack of a grill preheated to High. Grill for 8 minutes or until well marked, turning occasionally. Remove from the grill; cool slightly. Cut the corn from the cobs. Cut each beefsteak tomato and globe tomato into four 1/2-inch-thick slices for a total of 16 tomato slices. Sprinkle the tomato slices evenly with the salt. Alternate layers of tomatoes, avocado slices and bacon on each of 4 serving plates. Scatter the corn kernels evenly on the plates. Drizzle each stack with about 1 1/2 tablespoons of the buttermilk mixture and 1 teaspoon olive oil. Sprinkle with 1/4 teaspoon pepper.

NOTE: The presentation is prettier when using 2 different colors of tomatoes. Adding freshly cut corn kernels is fabulous and so easy because corn and tomatoes are in season at the same time and can be bought locally at your farmers' market.

Yield: 4 servings

Crunchy Slaw

1 cup shredded green cabbage
1 cup shredded red cabbage
1 cup chopped green onions
1 cup julienned carrots
1 cup frozen green peas
2 packages instant ramen noodles, crumbled
1 ounce sesame seeds, lightly toasted
1/2 cup slivered almonds, lightly toasted
1 cup vegetable oil
1 cup apple cider vinegar
Pinch of ginger

Combine the green cabbage, red cabbage, green onions, carrots, peas, ramen noodles, sesame seeds and almonds in a large bowl. Whisk the oil, vinegar and ginger in a bowl. Pour over the cabbage mixture and toss to mix. Chill at least until the peas have thawed.

Yield: 8 servings

Summer Roasted Corn Salad

CILANTRO VINAIGRETTE
5 tablespoons olive oil
2 tablespoons red wine vinegar
2 tablespoons minced fresh cilantro
1 teaspoon garlic powder
1/2 teaspoon salt
1/4 teaspoon freshly ground black pepper

SALAD
2 cups cherry tomatoes, cut into halves
2 cups roasted corn kernels
1 1/2 cups finely chopped peeled cucumber
1/2 small red onion, diced
2 avocados, diced
Fresh lemon juice
3/4 cup crumbled feta cheese
Salt and pepper to taste

For the Cilantro Vinaigrette, combine the olive oil, vinegar, cilantro, garlic powder, salt and pepper in a small sealable container; shake to mix well. Adjust the seasonings.

For the Salad, combine the tomatoes, corn, cucumber and onion in a large bowl. Sprinkle the avocados with lemon juice. Add the avocados and cheese to the salad. Drizzle with the Cilantro Vinaigrette and toss gently. Season with salt and pepper.

Yield: 8 servings

Fresh Kale Salad with Honey Peanut Dressing

1 large bunch of curly or lacinato kale, washed, trimmed and thinly sliced
1/4 cup apple cider vinegar
1/4 cup sesame seeds
1/4 cup extra-virgin olive oil
2 tablespoons honey
2 tablespoons organic smooth or chunky peanut butter
1 teaspoon tamari sauce
1/4 cup chopped parsley
Salt and freshly ground pepper to taste

Combine the kale and vinegar in a large salad bowl and toss using hands to coat all of the kale with vinegar. Let stand for 3 to 5 minutes or until the kale is tender. Toast the sesame seeds in a small pan over medium heat until fragrant. Whisk the olive oil, honey, peanut butter and tamari sauce in a small bowl. Stir in the parsley. Pour over the kale and toss to mix well. Sprinkle with the sesame seeds. Season with salt and pepper. Serve immediately or let stand for several minutes to allow the flavors to marry. May store leftovers, covered, in the refrigerator for up to 3 days.

Yield: 6 servings

Mixed Greens with Warm Goat Cheese and Candied Walnuts

CANDIED WALNUTS

1 large egg white

2 cups walnuts

1 cup sugar

CRANBERRY DRESSING

1/2 cup whole berry cranberry sauce

1/4 cup freshly squeezed orange juice

2 tablespoons balsamic vinegar

1 teaspoon sugar

1 teaspoon minced fresh ginger

1/4 teaspoon salt

1 tablespoon good-quality olive oil

WARM GOAT CHEESE MEDALLIONS

Goat cheese, cut into 1/2-inch slices

Olive oil

Breadcrumbs or panko breadcrumbs

SALAD

Red leaf lettuce

Spinach

2 red pears, sliced

For the Candied Walnuts, whisk the egg white until foamy. Stir in the walnuts and sugar until the walnuts are well coated. Spread evenly on a lightly greased foil-lined baking sheet. Bake at 350 degrees for 10 minutes. Stir gently. Bake for 10 minutes or until light golden brown. Cool completely.

For the Cranberry Dressing, combine the cranberry sauce, orange juice, vinegar, sugar, ginger and salt in a bowl. Whisk in the olive oil.

For the Warm Goat Cheese Medallions, dip the cheese slices into olive oil and coat with breadcrumbs. Arrange on a parchment-lined baking sheet. Broil for 1 minute per side, turning carefully.

For the Salad, mix lettuce and spinach in a salad bowl. Add the Cranberry Dressing and toss to mix. Arrange the pears, Warm Goat Cheese Medallions and Candied Walnuts on top.

Yield: 8 servings

Bacon, Lettuce and Tomato Salad with Buttermilk Blue Cheese Dressing

BUTTERMILK BLUE CHEESE DRESSING

1/2 cup mayonnaise

1/4 cup whole buttermilk

2 to 3 tablespoons crumbled blue cheese

1 tablespoon white vinegar

1 tablespoon fresh lemon juice

Freshly ground black pepper to taste

BLT SALAD

2 cups mixed greens

2 cups torn romaine lettuce

8 ounces bacon or pancetta, crisp-cooked and crumbled

2 large ripe tomatoes, cored, diced

2 tablespoons chopped red onion

2 tablespoons chopped fresh flat-leaf parsley

For the Buttermilk Blue Cheese Dressing, combine the mayonnaise, buttermilk, blue cheese, vinegar, lemon juice and pepper in a small bowl; mix well.

For the BLT Salad, combine the mixed greens, romaine, bacon, tomatoes and onion in a salad bowl. Sprinkle with the parsley. Serve with the Buttermilk Blue Cheese Dressing.

Yield: 6 to 8 servings

Bibb Lettuce with Hungarian Dressing

2 heads of Bibb or butter lettuce

1 cup buttermilk

2 tablespoons white wine vinegar

1 tablespoon sugar

1 teaspoon salt

Black pepper to taste

Tear the lettuce leaves into fourths; wash, drain and pat dry using paper towels. Combine the buttermilk, vinegar, sugar and salt in a salad bowl; mix well. Add the lettuce and toss to coat. Sprinkle with pepper.

Yield: 4 to 6 servings

Panda Pear Salad

1 large handful baby spinach
Thinly sliced red onion to taste
1 pear, cored and cut into 4 or 5 slices
1 tablespoon blue cheese crumbles
1 tablespoon dried cranberries
Toasted Sesame Vinaigrette (recipe below)
1 teaspoon sesame seeds

Combine the spinach, onion, pear, blue cheese and dried cranberries in a salad bowl. Toss with 1 to 2 ounces of the Toasted Sesame Vinaigrette. Arrange the salad on a plate. Sprinkle with the sesame seeds.

Yield: 1 serving

FLOWER OF THE CAROLINAS

The beauty of the area was chronicled early in the 1700s as "the flower of the Carolinas," and the richness of the land allowed farmers and land owners to gain affluence and prosperity.

Toasted Sesame Vinaigrette

1/2 cup extra-virgin olive oil
3 tablespoons aged balsamic vinegar
3 tablespoons soy sauce
1 clove of garlic, minced
1 teaspoon minced shallot
1 heaping teaspoon Dijon mustard
1 teaspoon toasted sesame oil

Combine the olive oil, vinegar, soy sauce, garlic, shallot, mustard and sesame oil in a canning jar; secure the lid. Shake vigorously until emulsified.

Mango Orzo Salad

DIJON VINAIGRETTE
6 tablespoons extra-virgin olive oil
2 tablespoons white wine vinegar
1 tablespoon Dijon mustard
2 teaspoons sugar
Salt and pepper to taste

SALAD
1/2 cup whole wheat orzo
1 mango, peeled and cubed
1 red bell pepper, diced
1 small onion, diced
1 small cucumber, diced
1 (15-ounce) can chickpeas, drained and rinsed
3 tablespoons chopped fresh basil and/or tarragon
1 handful fresh spinach, torn into bite-size pieces
1/4 cup pine nuts, toasted

For the Dijon Vinaigrette, combine the olive oil, vinegar, mustard, sugar, salt and pepper in a jar with a tight-fitting lid. Cover and shake to blend.

For the Salad, cook the orzo according to the package directions; cool. Combine the orzo, mango, bell pepper, onion, cucumber and chickpeas in a large salad bowl. Stir in the basil and/or tarragon, spinach and pine nuts. Pour the Dijon Vinaigrette over the salad and toss to coat. Chill for 1 hour to overnight. It's even better the second day!

Yield: 4 servings

SUMMER SELTZER

This Summer Seltzer is the perfect complement to the light and fruity orzo salad. Fill a glass with ice. Add 1/2 jigger of lemon juice, 1 jigger of vodka and 1 1/2 jiggers of Dekuyper triple sec. Add enough lemon-lime seltzer water to fill the glass. Garnish with slices of lemon and/or lime.

Kale and Quinoa with Lemon Dijon Vinaigrette

LEMON DIJON VINAIGRETTE
1/4 cup extra-virgin olive oil
2 tablespoons fresh lemon juice
1 1/2 teaspoons Dijon mustard
1/4 teaspoon freshly ground black pepper

SALAD
1 cup quinoa
1 3/4 cups water
1 bunch of kale
1/2 cup diced cucumber
1/2 cup diced red bell pepper
1/4 cup crumbled feta cheese
1/2 to 3/4 cup roasted sunflower seeds
Cherry tomato halves for garnish

For the Lemon Dijon Vinaigrette, combine the olive oil, lemon juice, mustard and pepper in a small bowl. Whisk until well blended.

For the Salad, cook the quinoa in the water according to the package directions, simmering for 15 to 20 minutes or until tender; drain if needed. Let stand to cool. Remove and discard the center stems of the kale. Cut the kale chiffonade-style and cut the strips in half. Place in a large salad bowl. Add the cucumber and bell pepper. Add the quinoa, cheese and sunflower seeds. Drizzle the Lemon Dijon Vinaigrette over the salad and toss to mix. Store, covered, in the refrigerator for 1 week or longer. Serve cold or at room temperature. Garnish with cherry tomato halves.

Yield: 4 to 6 servings

Quinoa Vegetable Salad

This healthy, make-ahead recipe comes from Jenny Levy, head coach of women's lacrosse at the University of North Carolina at Chapel Hill.

LIME VINAIGRETTE
1/2 cup olive oil
2 tablespoons red wine vinegar
2 tablespoons fresh lime juice
2 teaspoons ground cumin
1 teaspoon chili powder

SALAD
1 cup quinoa
Chicken stock
1 can black beans, rinsed and drained
1 cup fresh corn kernels
1 red bell pepper, diced
1 yellow, green, or orange bell pepper, diced
1/2 cup diagonally sliced green onions
1/2 cup chopped fresh cilantro
Salt and pepper to taste

For the Lime Vinaigrette, combine the olive oil, vinegar, lime juice, cumin and chili powder in a bowl and whisk to mix well.

For the Salad, prepare the quinoa according to the package directions, using chicken stock for the liquid; cool slightly. Place in a large bowl. Add the Lime Vinaigrette and toss to mix. Let cool to room temperature. Stir in the beans, corn, red bell pepper, yellow bell pepper, green onions and cilantro. Season with salt and pepper. Chill, covered, until serving time.

Yield: 8 to 10 servings

Sally's Spinach Salad

This salad was a favorite of the Taste of Tobacco Road *Committee during the days spent shooting the photographs included in the book. Sally Graham, mother of Core Committee Member Sarah Motsinger, is a sustainer in the Junior League of Durham and Orange Counties. Sally donated her beautiful home as the backdrop for* Taste's *photography.*

SPINACH SALAD VINAIGRETTE

1 cup extra-virgin olive oil
1/3 cup red wine vinegar
1/4 cup sugar
2 teaspoons Dijon mustard
Salt and pepper to taste

SPINACH SALAD

3 cups spinach, washed and dried
6 slices crisp-fried bacon, crumbled
4 hard-cooked eggs, peeled and sliced
8 ounces fresh mushrooms, sliced
1 medium red onion, sliced
Croutons (optional)

For the Spinach Salad Vinaigrette, combine the olive oil, vinegar, sugar, mustard, salt and pepper in a glass container with a lid. Shake until all the ingredients are well mixed.

For the Spinach Salad, combine the spinach, bacon, eggs, mushrooms, onion and croutons in a large serving bowl. Drizzle the Spinach Salad Vinaigrette over the salad and toss to mix.

Yield: 6 servings

Festive Fall Salad

TARRAGON VINAIGRETTE

3 tablespoons olive oil or liquid coconut oil

1 tablespoon red wine vinegar

1 teaspoon dried tarragon

Salt and pepper to taste

SALAD

2 cups butternut squash, peeled, seeded
and cut into cubes

Vegetable oil

1 cup pomegranate seeds

3 tablespoons goat cheese

5 ounces mixed green lettuces

For the Tarragon Vinaigrette, combine the olive oil, vinegar, tarragon, salt and pepper in a small bowl and whisk until well blended.

For the Salad, toss the squash with a small amount of oil to coat in a bowl. Spread on a roasting pan. Bake at 400 degrees for about 40 minutes, tossing occasionally; cool. Combine with the pomegranate seeds, goat cheese and lettuces in a large bowl. Add the Tarragon Vinaigrette to the salad and toss to coat.

Yield: 6 servings

Roasted Tomato and Butter Bean Salad

3 to 4 pounds mixed tomatoes,
such as heirloom, grape, cherry,
beefsteak and Roma

2 tablespoons olive oil

Salt and pepper to taste

3 tablespoons capers

1 tablespoon olive oil

2 cups cooked butter beans

1 large bunch of fresh basil, torn

1 tablespoon lemon zest (optional)

1 tablespoon olive oil

Cut the tomatoes into bite-size slices, cubes or quarters. Mix half the tomatoes with 2 tablespoons olive oil. Sprinkle with salt and pepper. Arrange on a baking sheet. Roast at 425 degrees for 20 minutes. Sauté the capers in 1 tablespoon olive oil in a skillet over medium heat for 2 to 3 minutes. Combine the roasted tomatoes, fresh tomatoes, butter beans, basil, capers and lemon zest in a large bowl and toss to mix. Drizzle with 1 tablespoon olive oil. Season with salt and pepper.

Yield: 6 servings

Egg Salad Wraps

6 hard-cooked eggs, cooled, peeled and diced
4 ounces smoked salmon filets, flaked
1 rib of celery, diced
1/3 cup plain yogurt
3 tablespoons good-quality mustard
1 tablespoon chopped fresh basil, or 1 teaspoon dried basil
1/2 to 1 teaspoon hot sauce (optional)
Salt and pepper to taste
6 collard green leaves

Combine the eggs, salmon, celery, yogurt, mustard, basil, hot sauce, salt and pepper in a bowl; mix well. Remove the spines from the collard green leaves about halfway down each leaf. Microwave for 10 to 15 seconds if the collard greens are tough. Fold the ends of each leaf together to make a cup. Fill each with 1 to 2 tablespoonfuls of the egg salad; roll up toward the top, folding in one side to hold in the salad.

Yield: 6 servings

Tarragon and Rosemary Chicken Salad

OLIVE OIL MAYONNAISE

1 egg yolk
1 tablespoon vinegar or lemon juice
1 tablespoon Dijon mustard
Pinch of salt
1 to 2 cups olive oil

CHICKEN SALAD

3 pounds boneless skinless chicken breasts
1 1/2 cups chopped celery
1 1/2 cups halved or quartered seedless grapes
3/4 cup walnuts (optional)
1 tablespoon chopped rosemary
1 tablespoon tarragon
1/4 cup Dijon mustard
Salt and pepper to taste

For the Olive Oil Mayonnaise, combine the egg yolk, vinegar, mustard and salt in a food processor. Pulse once or twice to mix. Process on Low while adding the olive oil very gradually until the mixture resembles mayonnaise. Let stand for 15 to 20 minutes before refrigerating or serve immediately.

For the Chicken Salad, bake the chicken breasts in a baking pan at 350 degrees for 30 minutes or until the juices run clear; cool. Cut into 1-inch cubes to make about 3 cups. Place in a large bowl. Add the celery, grapes, walnuts, rosemary and tarragon; mix lightly. Add the Olive Oil Mayonnaise, mustard, salt and pepper; mix well.

NOTE: Do not use extra-virgin olive oil as the resulting taste will be too strong.

Yield: 7 to 8 cups

HOMEGROWN HERBS AND SPICES

Growing your own herbs and spices is a simple way to add edible plants to your diet. Many herbs and spices are extremely versatile, growing well in the garden or even small containers. The first step to growing your own? Deciding what you want to grow and determining where you want to plant them. After planting, water at least once a week and harvest when ready to give your taste buds a fresh treat straight from your own garden.

Firebirds' Grilled Shrimp and Strawberry Salad

FIREBIRDS WOOD FIRED GRILL

Firebirds Wood Fired Grill is known for classic American, wood fired grilled entrées. Located at The Streets of Southpoint, Firebirds features a large variety of bold selections prepared in-house—seared over local North Carolina hickory, oak, or pecan wood. Firebirds Wood Fired Grill was named one of the ten 2014 "Breakout Brands" by *Nation's Restaurant News*. The sweet and spicy notes in this recipe, paired with wood fired shrimp, will transport you no matter where you enjoy it.

SPICED PECANS
1 pound broken pecans
3 tablespoons butter, melted
1/3 cup packed brown sugar
1/2 teaspoon ancho chile powder

SALAD
28 shrimp, cleaned, deveined and tails removed
Salt and pepper to taste
8 cups mixed greens
1 cup julienned jicama
3 cups sliced strawberries
1 cup goat cheese crumbles
8 ounces balsamic vinaigrette salad dressing

For the Spiced Pecans, combine the pecans, butter, brown sugar and chile powder in a bowl; mix well. Spread in a single layer on a baking sheet. Bake at 350 degrees for 10 to 15 minutes or until toasted, stirring every 2 minutes; cool. Store in an airtight container for up to 2 weeks.

For the Salad, thread the shrimp onto skewers. Sprinkle both sides with salt and pepper. Grill over hot coals for 3 minutes per side or until the shrimp turn pink and are cooked through. Remove the shrimp from the skewers. Combine the mixed greens, jicama, 1 cup of the Spiced Pecans, strawberries and goat cheese in a large bowl; toss lightly. Add the vinaigrette; toss to mix. Place on salad plates. Divide the shrimp evenly among the salads. Grab a fork and dig in!

NOTE: If using wooden skewers, let soak in water for 10 minutes prior to using to prevent sticking.

Yield: 4 servings

Carolina Shrimp Salad

Made with leftovers from the weekend's seafood dock purchases, this shrimp salad is a Carolina favorite for lazy Sunday afternoons spent on the shore. Serve with crackers and celery for a perfect lunch.

1 pound fresh shrimp in the shell, rinsed
2 cloves of garlic
Celery leaves to taste
Red bell pepper to taste
$1/2$ to 1 lemon
Garlic salt to taste
Chopped celery to taste
Mayonnaise

Bring a large pot of water to a boil. Add the shrimp, garlic, celery leaves and bell pepper. Cook for about 3 minutes or until the shrimp turn pink; drain. Shell and devein the shrimp; cut into pieces and place in a bowl. Squeeze the lemon juice over the shrimp. Sprinkle with garlic salt. Add chopped celery and enough mayonnaise to hold the mixture together, mixing lightly.

Yield: 3 or 4 servings

Shrimp and Asparagus Salad

1 fennel bulb with fronds
1 pound medium shrimp, shelled and deveined
Salt and freshly ground pepper to taste
Olive oil for sautéing
1 bunch of asparagus
1/4 cup extra-virgin olive oil
3 tablespoons red wine vinegar
1/2 teaspoon fennel seeds, crushed
1 clove of garlic, minced (about 1/2 teaspoon)
1/2 teaspoon kosher salt
1 (15-ounce) can cannellini beans
1/2 cup diced red onion

Cut the stems and feathery fronds from the fennel bulb. Reserve the fronds; discard the outer layers and any discolored areas of the bulb. Cut the bulb lengthwise into fourths and discard any tough areas. Soak in ice water to cover in a bowl for 30 minutes; drain well. Cut into 1/4-inch pieces to make about 2 cups. Finely chop enough of the reserved fronds to yield 1/2 cup.

Season the shrimp with salt and pepper to taste and sauté in a small amount of olive oil in a skillet until pink and cooked through. Remove to a plate to cool. Cut into bite-size pieces. Trim the woody ends of the asparagus and chop the asparagus into 1-inch pieces. Sauté in the same skillet until tender-crisp, adding additional olive oil if needed. Let stand to cool.

Whisk 1/4 cup olive oil, vinegar, fennel seeds, garlic, 1/2 teaspoon salt and pepper to taste in a large bowl until well blended. Add the chopped fennel bulb, fronds, shrimp, asparagus, beans and onion. Stir gently until well mixed. Serve immediately.

Yield: 4 to 6 servings

Watermelon Salad

2 tablespoons fresh lemon juice
2 tablespoons fresh lime juice
Coarsely ground salt and freshly ground pepper to taste
1 (4-pound) seedless watermelon, cut into 1-inch cubes
1 pint fresh blueberries
10 ounces feta cheese, broken or cut into 1-inch cubes
1 cup torn fresh basil leaves

Combine the lemon juice, lime juice, salt and pepper in a small bowl and mix well. Combine the watermelon, blueberries, cheese and basil in a large bowl. Drizzle with the lemon juice mixture and toss to coat. Serve immediately. May substitute mint for the basil and/or cucumber chunks for the blueberries.

NOTE: For an appetizer presentation, alternate the blueberries, watermelon, cheese and untorn basil leaves on soaked skewers and drizzle with the lemon juice mixture just before serving.

Yield: 8 to 10 servings

WATERMELON

The watermelon is an annual plant that is thought to have originated in South Africa. Containing over 92 percent water, the vine fruit is not only a source of vitamin C, but is a staple in North Carolina homes during the summer. Whether in slices during a barbecue or prepared in a watermelon cocktail, the fruit can be eaten raw or cooked and is the most consumed melon in the United States.

Taste the Action—Pick a Side

SIDE DISHES

Tobacco Road Sports and Rivalries

Although not an actual geographical location, Tobacco Road symbolizes much more to those who live here and fans of the four most historic universities in the region. It was home to the first football game played south of the Mason-Dixon line, and it is home to some of the most well-known rivalries in college athletics.

As the rivalry continued to grow, much like other areas in the South, football was king. It was almost ten years later when a new sport showed up around Tobacco Road: basketball. Fourteen years after Dr. James Naismith founded basketball, this new "sport" suddenly attracted interest from football-loving Trinity College, with the help of athletic director Wilber Wade Card. Card brought the game to Durham in 1906, paving the way for a basketball history that would include Eddie Cameron, Vic Bubas, Mike Krzyzewski, Dean Smith, and Roy Williams.

However, it wasn't until 1935, when the plans for what became Cameron Indoor Stadium were sketched out on a matchbook, that the Tobacco Road truly gained a basketball shrine. The largest of its kind at the time, Cameron was expected to hold close to 8,800 fans, while UNC's new facility was built to hold only 4,000, and NC State's, 3,500. When a crowd of 8,000 fans— still 800 under capacity—turned out for the arena's 1940 opening game, one columnist predicted that the new stadium would never be filled. Little did he know the level of basketball fever that was on the horizon!

Fast-forward almost sixty-five years, and the rivalry between the "Big Four" is still as prominent as ever. Overall, Duke, UNC, Wake Forest, and NC State have sixty-five NCAA Division 1 national team championships in men's and women's sports, and they have also won at least sixty-one NCAA Division 1 individual national championships in men's and women's sports. UNC's forty team championships are the most in the ACC. Over time, these five schools established deep-rooted rivalries and ultimately became the landscape of Tobacco Road.

Maple Pecan Roasted Brussels Sprouts

2 pounds Brussels sprouts
1/2 cup pecans
6 slices bacon
3 tablespoons extra-virgin olive oil
1 teaspoon kosher salt
1/2 teaspoon pepper
2 1/2 tablespoons balsamic vinegar
1 tablespoon pure maple syrup

Remove and discard the stems and outer leaves from the Brussels sprouts. Cut the Brussels sprouts into halves. Bake the pecans on a foil-lined baking sheet at 350 degrees for 5 minutes or until lightly toasted. Remove the pecans to a cutting board and chop coarsely. Fry the bacon in a skillet, or place on a baking sheet and bake at 400 degrees for 12 to 20 minutes, rotating the baking sheet once for even cooking. Drain the bacon on paper towels, reserving the drippings. Increase the oven temperature to 425 degrees. Arrange the Brussels sprouts on a foil-lined baking sheet. Drizzle with the reserved bacon drippings and olive oil. Sprinkle with the salt and pepper. Roast for 20 minutes or until tender and caramelized, turning the Brussels sprouts after 10 minutes for even browning. Toss with the vinegar and maple syrup to coat evenly. Adjust the seasonings. Serve hot or at room temperature, sprinkling with the pecans and bacon just before serving.

Yield: 6 servings

Stewed Greek Green Beans

This recipe comes from UNC athletic director Bubba Cunningham and his wife, Tina, who are key players in the athletic and nonprofit communities in Durham and Orange Counties. Passed down through many generations, this recipe originated with the Cunningham family's grandmother, who emigrated from Greece in the 1930s.

1 large onion, chopped
1/2 cup extra-virgin olive oil
2 pounds green beans, rinsed and trimmed
1 (14-ounce) can diced tomatoes
10 peeled baby carrots
1 or 2 potatoes, peeled and cubed
Salt and pepper to taste
Tomato sauce (optional)

Sauté the onion in the olive oil in a large saucepan over medium-high heat until browned. Add the green beans, tomatoes, carrots, potatoes, salt and pepper; mix well. Simmer, covered, for 1 hour or until the vegetables are tender. Add enough tomato sauce to moisten if the mixture becomes too dry. Serve with steak, chicken, pork or fish. This dish is great with crusty bread.

NOTE: For the best flavor, do not use light olive oil.

Yield: 6 servings

Tangy Marinated Carrots

5 cups sliced fresh carrots (about 2 bunches)
1 medium onion, cut into rings
1 small green bell pepper, sliced
1 (10-ounce) can tomato soup
1/2 cup vegetable oil
1 cup sugar

3/4 cup apple cider vinegar
1 teaspoon prepared mustard
1 teaspoon Worcestershire sauce
1 teaspoon salt
1 teaspoon pepper

Cook the carrots in boiling water to cover in a saucepan for 20 minutes; drain and cool. Combine the carrots, onion and bell pepper in a large bowl. Mix the tomato soup, vegetable oil, sugar, vinegar, mustard, Worcestershire sauce, salt and pepper in a bowl. Pour over the vegetable mixture. Marinate, covered, in the refrigerator overnight. May store in the refrigerator for several days to 1 week. The carrots get better with time.

Yield: 8 servings

Slow Cooker Collards

6 ounces light turkey or ham (optional)
2 (16-ounce) bunches of collard greens, chopped
1 large onion, chopped
1 (32-ounce) carton 99-percent fat-free chicken broth

2 teaspoons sugar
1 teaspoon salt (optional)
1/4 cup apple cider vinegar
1/2 tablespoon extra-virgin olive oil
Garlic powder, chili powder and/or crushed red pepper to taste

Place the turkey in a slow cooker. Add the collards and onion in multiple layers. Add 3/4 of the broth. Cook, covered, on High for 45 minutes or until the collards are cooked down slightly. Mix the remaining broth, sugar, salt, vinegar and olive oil in a bowl. Add garlic powder, chili powder and/or crushed red pepper. Pour over the collards and stir to mix well. Cook for 5 hours or until the collards have reached the desired consistency, stirring occasionally.

Yield: 6 servings

Gratinéed Cauliflower

4 cloves of garlic, minced
6 tablespoons unsalted butter
4 ounces thinly sliced prosciutto,
   cut into thin strips
Florets of 1 large head cauliflower, cut
   lengthwise into 1/4-inch slices

2 tablespoons unbleached all-purpose flour
1 1/2 cups heavy whipping cream
Pinch of cayenne pepper
Salt and black pepper to taste
1 1/2 cups grated Swiss cheese
1/2 cup chopped fresh parsley

Sauté the garlic in the butter in a large skillet over medium-high heat for 2 minutes. Add the prosciutto. Sauté for 2 minutes. Add the cauliflower. Cook for 3 to 4 minutes or just until tender. Stir in the flour. Add the cream and mix well. Season with cayenne pepper, salt and black pepper. Bring to a boil; remove from the heat. Pour into an au gratin dish. Top with the cheese and parsley. Bake at 350 degrees for 30 minutes or until lightly browned and bubbly. Serve immediately.

   Yield: 6 servings

Corn Soufflé

1/2 cup butter
2 cups fresh corn kernels
   (6 to 8 ears of corn)
6 eggs, beaten
1 tablespoon sugar

1/2 teaspoon salt
1/2 teaspoon black pepper
1/4 teaspoon cayenne pepper
2 cups half-and-half

Melt the butter in a large saucepan over medium-low heat. Stir in the corn. Remove from the heat. Fold in the eggs, sugar, salt, black pepper, cayenne pepper and half-and-half. Spoon into a warmed 2-quart casserole dish. Bake at 325 degrees for 1 hour or until set and a knife inserted near the center comes out clean.

   Yield: 6 servings

Roasted Parsnips with Cilantro Dipping Sauce

CILANTRO DIPPING SAUCE

1 bunch of cilantro, chopped

Juice and grated zest of 1 lime

1 small clove of garlic, minced

1 chili in adobo sauce, or 1 tablespoon
    adobo sauce

3 tablespoons Greek yogurt

1 teaspoon sugar

1/2 teaspoon salt

1/2 teaspoon pepper

PARSNIPS

4 to 5 pounds parsnips

2 tablespoons vegetable oil

1 tablespoon mild, medium or
    hot curry paste

1/2 tablespoon ground cumin

1 tablespoon ground turmeric

1 teaspoon salt

1 teaspoon pepper

For the Cilantro Dipping Sauce, combine the cilantro, lime juice, lime zest, garlic, chili, yogurt, sugar, salt and pepper in a food processor or blender. Process until thick and smooth.

For the Parsnips, cut the parsnips into 1/2 x 2-inch sticks. Place in a microwave-safe bowl. Add a small amount of water and cover with a plate. Microwave on High for 7 minutes; drain. Spread on a baking sheet. Pat dry with paper towels. Let stand to cool slightly. Combine the oil, curry paste, cumin, turmeric, salt and pepper in a large bowl. Add the parsnips and toss to coat thoroughly. Return to the baking sheet or spread onto 2 baking sheets to prevent overcrowding. Bake at 425 degrees for 30 to 45 minutes or until tender. Serve with the Cilantro Dipping Sauce.

Yield: 6 to 8 servings

Maple Baked Onions

6 large Vidalia onions, cut into $1/2$-inch slices
$1/3$ cup maple syrup
4 tablespoons butter, melted

Layer the Vidalia onions in a 9×13-inch baking dish. Drizzle with a mixture of the maple syrup and butter. Bake at 425 degrees for 40 to 45 minutes or until the onions are tender and glazed.

Yield: 6 servings

Loaded Mashed Potato Casserole

5 pounds russet potatoes, peeled and
   chopped into small pieces
4 tablespoons butter, softened
8 ounces sour cream

8 ounces cream cheese, softened
3 cups shredded sharp Cheddar cheese
1 (3-ounce) package real bacon pieces
Salt and pepper to taste

Cook the potatoes in boiling water to cover in a large saucepan until tender and easily pierced using a fork; drain. Transfer to a mixing bowl. Add the butter, sour cream and cream cheese. Beat until blended and smooth. Fold in the cheese, bacon, salt and pepper. Spoon into a greased $8 1/2 \times 11$-inch casserole dish. Bake at 350 degrees for 20 minutes.

Yield: 8 to 10 servings

White Cheddar and Tarragon Potato Gratin

3 pounds Yukon Gold potatoes, peeled
   and cut into 1/8-inch slices
2 teaspoons salt
1 teaspoon pepper
2 1/2 teaspoons dried tarragon

1 1/2 cups packed grated white Cheddar
   cheese (about 6 ounces)
1 cup heavy whipping cream
1 cup dry white wine

Layer 1/3 of the potatoes in a buttered 9 x 13-inch glass baking dish, overlapping the slices slightly. Sprinkle with 2/3 teaspoon salt, 1/3 teaspoon pepper, rounded 3/4 teaspoon tarragon and 1/2 cup cheese. Repeat the potato, salt, pepper, tarragon and cheese layers 2 times. Whisk the cream and wine in a medium bowl until blended. Pour over the layers. Bake, uncovered, at 400 degrees for 1 hour or until the potatoes are easily pierced using a knife and the top is golden brown. Let stand for 5 minutes before serving.

Yield: 6 to 8 servings

Sauté of Spinach and Apples

2 (6-ounce) packages fresh spinach
2 tablespoons olive oil
1 clove of garlic, chopped
1 Granny Smith apple, cored and chopped

Cook the spinach in the olive oil in a skillet over medium-high heat just until the spinach begins to wilt, turning several times using tongs. Add the garlic and cook until the spinach is wilted. Add the apple and cook for 1 minute longer.

Yield: 6 servings

Sweet Potato Fries

SWEET-AND-SPICY MUSTARD

1 cup apple cider vinegar
1 cup sugar

5 eggs
1 (4-ounce) can dry mustard

SWEET POTATO FRIES

3 large North Carolina sweet potatoes
3 tablespoons olive oil
3 cloves of garlic, minced
1 teaspoon kosher salt
1/2 teaspoon crushed red pepper

1/4 teaspoon paprika
1/4 teaspoon chili powder
1/4 teaspoon dried oregano
Freshly ground pepper to taste
Nonstick cooking spray

For the Sweet-and-Spicy Mustard, combine the vinegar, sugar, eggs and dry mustard in a medium saucepan. Blend using an immersion blender or process in a food processor until smooth. Cook over medium-low heat until thickened, stirring constantly; remove from the heat. Fill sterilized canning jars 2/3 full. Seal and process in a hot water bath. Store in a cool, dry place for up to 12 months. Store opened jars in the refrigerator.

For the Sweet Potato Fries, chop the sweet potatoes into 1-inch or smaller cubes; do not peel. Combine the sweet potatoes, olive oil, garlic, salt, crushed red pepper, paprika, chili powder, oregano and pepper in a large bowl and toss to coat. Spread in a baking dish or on a baking sheet sprayed with nonstick cooking spray. Bake at 425 degrees for 30 minutes or until crispy, stirring after 15 minutes. Serve with Sweet-and-Spicy Mustard as the perfect accompaniment.

NOTE: The higher oven temperature makes the fries crispier.

Yield: 6 to 8 servings

Sweet Potato, Onion and Cheese Tart

CHICKPEA CRUST

1 2/3 cups chickpea flour
1/4 teaspoon salt

1/4 cup olive oil
1/2 cup cold water

TART

1 1/2 to 2 pounds sweet potatoes, cut into
   3/4-inch cubes
1 medium red onion, diced
1/4 teaspoon cracked pepper
1/2 teaspoon herb blend, such as herbes de
   Provence or Italian herb blend
1/2 teaspoon minced garlic

2 tablespoons olive oil
8 ounces shredded Gruyère cheese
4 eggs
1 cup milk
1/2 cup sour cream or plain yogurt
1 teaspoon dried rosemary
1/4 teaspoon salt

For the Chickpea Crust, combine the chickpea flour and salt in a medium bowl. Add the olive oil gradually, stirring until crumbly. Add the water gradually, stirring to form a soft dough. Press over the bottom and side of a greased tart pan. Prick the bottom of the crust 6 or 8 times using a fork. Bake at 425 degrees for 10 minutes; cool.

For the Tart, combine the sweet potatoes, onion, pepper, herb blend, garlic and olive oil in a large bowl and toss to coat. Spread in a single layer in a baking pan. Roast at 425 degrees for 20 to 30 minutes or until the sweet potatoes are tender. Spoon half the sweet potato mixture over the bottom of the Chickpea Crust. Sprinkle with half the cheese. Repeat the layers. Pour a mixture of the eggs, milk, sour cream, rosemary and salt carefully over the top. Bake at 350 degrees or 35 to 40 minutes or until set. Cool on a wire rack for 15 minutes. Cut into wedges to serve.

   Yield: 8 servings

Southern Sweet Potato Casserole

3 cups cooked coarsely chopped
   sweet potatoes
1 cup sugar
2 eggs
1 teaspoon vanilla extract
1/2 cup butter, softened

1/3 cup milk
1 cup packed brown sugar
1 cup coarsely chopped pecans
1/3 cup flour
1/3 cup butter, melted

Combine the sweet potatoes, sugar and eggs in a large mixing bowl; beat until blended. Add the vanilla, softened butter and milk; beat until blended. Spoon into a greased 9×13-inch baking dish. Combine the brown sugar, pecans, flour and melted butter in a small bowl; mix until crumbly. Sprinkle evenly over the potatoes. Bake at 350 degrees for 35 to 40 minutes or until hot and bubbly.

Yield: 8 servings

Marinated Vegetables

1 bunch of broccoli, cut into small pieces
1 head of cauliflower, cut into small pieces
1 yellow squash, sliced
1 medium green bell pepper,
   finely chopped
5 spring onions, finely chopped
15 medium fresh mushrooms, sliced

15 cherry tomatoes
1/2 cup vegetable oil
1 cup sugar
3/4 cup vinegar
1 teaspoon dry mustard
1 teaspoon salt
1 teaspoon celery seed

Combine the broccoli, cauliflower, squash, bell pepper, spring onions, mushrooms and tomatoes in a large bowl. Combine the oil, sugar, vinegar, dry mustard, salt and celery seed in a small saucepan. Cook over medium heat until the sugar is dissolved, stirring frequently; cool. Pour over the vegetables; mix well. Chill, covered, in the refrigerator for 24 hours, stirring occasionally.

Yield: 8 to 12 servings

Zucchini Cakes with Tomato Coulis

This dish is a local favorite in the late summer when farmers' markets are bursting with fresh tomatoes, garlic, basil and zucchini. The chilled coulis is the perfect way to cool off in the hot Carolina summers.

TOMATO COULIS

2 large tomatoes, seeded and
    coarsely chopped
1/4 cup coarsely chopped sun-dried
    tomatoes

1/2 cup chopped fresh basil
Salt and pepper to taste

ZUCCHINI CAKES

2 cups shredded zucchini
1 cup shredded Cheddar cheese or
    mozzarella cheese
3/4 cup (scant) chickpea flour or other flour
3 or 4 scallions, green and white parts
    chopped

1 egg, beaten
1 teaspoon dried basil
1/2 teaspoon dried oregano
1/2 teaspoon dried thyme
1 clove of garlic, minced
Salt and pepper to taste

For the Tomato Coulis, combine the tomatoes, sun-dried tomatoes, basil, salt and pepper in a food processor. Pulse 15 to 20 times. Chill overnight.

For the Zucchini Cakes, wrap the zucchini in a kitchen towel. Squeeze until the liquid is removed. Combine the zucchini, cheese, flour, scallions, egg, basil, oregano, thyme, garlic, salt and pepper in a large bowl; mix well to make a thick, sticky dough. Shape into 2- to 2 1/2-inch patties. Fry in a skillet over medium heat for 4 to 5 minutes per side. Top each zucchini cake with a spoonful of the chilled Tomato Coulis. Serve immediately.

Yield: 2 dozen

Hot Cranberry Casserole

3 cups chopped apples
2 cups whole fresh cranberries
Nonstick cooking spray
1 teaspoon lemon juice
1 1/2 cups sugar
1 1/3 cups quick-cooking oats
1 cup chopped walnuts
1/3 cup packed brown sugar
1/2 cup margarine, melted

Combine the apples and cranberries in a 2-quart casserole dish sprayed with nonstick cooking spray. Sprinkle with the lemon juice. Spoon the sugar over the top to cover. Combine the oats, walnuts, brown sugar and margarine in a medium bowl. Mix just until moistened. Sprinkle over the fruit. Bake, uncovered, at 325 degrees for 1 1/4 hours.

NOTE: For a summer variation, substitute cherries and almond flavoring for the cranberries and lemon juice.

Yield: 6 to 8 servings

Bahamian Macaroni and Cheese

1 (16-ounce) package ziti
1/2 medium onion, diced
1/2 green bell pepper, diced
1 rib of celery, diced
4 tablespoons butter
1 pound Cheddar cheese, grated
3 eggs, beaten
1/4 cup hot red pepper sauce
2 (12-ounce) cans evaporated milk
Salt to taste
Paprika to taste

Cook the ziti according to the package directions for 15 minutes; drain. Sauté the onion, bell pepper and celery in the butter in a skillet until tender. Reserve a small amount of the cheese. Add the onion mixture, remaining cheese, eggs, hot sauce, evaporated milk and salt to the ziti in a large bowl; mix well. Spoon into a greased baking dish. Top with the reserved cheese; sprinkle with paprika. Bake at 350 degrees for 30 minutes or until golden brown.

Yield: 8 servings

BAHAMA

In 1981, when Durham County was formed from the eastern half of Orange County, a new name was created for the settlement to acknowledge the three prominent families that resided there. The Balls, The Harrises, and The Mangums make up the name Bahama (buh-HAY-muh).

Better Than Take-Out Fried Rice

STIR-FRY SAUCE

2 tablespoons cornstarch
2 1/2 tablespoons brown sugar
1/8 teaspoon crushed red pepper or
    cayenne pepper
1/2 cup light corn syrup
1/2 cup soy sauce

2 tablespoons cooking sherry
1 tablespoon toasted sesame oil
1 tablespoon rice vinegar
1 1/2 teaspoons minced garlic
1 1/2 teaspoons ground ginger

FRIED RICE

1 cup frozen peas and carrots
1 white onion, diced
2 cloves of garlic, minced
3 tablespoons sesame oil
2 eggs

Water chestnuts, sesame seeds and sliced
    green onions (optional)
4 cups cooked rice
1 1/2 pounds chopped cooked chicken
1 1/4 cups soy sauce

For the Stir-Fry Sauce, combine the cornstarch, brown sugar and crushed red pepper in a small saucepan. Add the corn syrup, soy sauce, cooking sherry, toasted sesame oil, rice vinegar, garlic and ginger; mix well. Bring to a boil over medium heat, stirring occasionally. Boil for 1 minute. Simmer for 1 to 2 minutes longer or until thickened and syrupy, stirring frequently. Store, covered, in the refrigerator for up to 2 weeks.

For the Fried Rice, sauté the peas and carrots, onion and garlic in the sesame oil in a large skillet over medium-high heat until tender. Add the eggs. Cook until the eggs are cooked through, stirring constantly to mix throughout. Stir in the water chestnuts, sesame seeds and green onions. Add the rice, chicken and soy sauce, stirring to mix well; remove from the heat. Drizzle with the Stir-Fry Sauce just before serving.

    Yield: 8 to 10 servings

Squash Dressing

1 (8-ounce) package corn muffin mix
4 cups chopped yellow squash
1/2 cup chopped onion
1/2 cup chopped celery
1/2 cup chopped green bell pepper
1/2 cup butter
1 (10-ounce) can cream of chicken soup
1 cup milk
1 teaspoon salt
1/2 teaspoon pepper

Prepare and bake the corn muffins according to the package directions; cool. Crumble into a large bowl. Cook the squash in 1/2-inch of boiling water in a large covered saucepan for 3 to 5 minutes or until tender-crisp; drain. Add the squash to the corn muffins. Sauté the onion, celery and bell pepper in the butter in a skillet until tender. Add to the squash mixture and mix well. Combine the soup, milk, salt and pepper in a small bowl; mix well. Stir into the squash mixture. Spoon into a greased 7×11-inch baking dish. Bake at 350 degrees for 40 to 45 minutes or until golden brown.

Yield: 6 servings

RED WINE SPICED SANGRIA

To make Red Wine Spiced Sangria, combine 1 cup apple juice, 1/3 cup triple sec, 1/4 cup sugar, 4 whole cloves, 1 blood orange or navel orange, cut into 1/4-inch slices, 1 lemon, cut into 1/4-inch slices, 2 (3-inch) cinnamon sticks, 1 Bartlett pear, cut into 1/2-inch cubes, and 1 (750-mL) bottle of fruity red wine in a large pitcher. Stir until the sugar is dissolved. Chill, covered, for 4 hours to overnight. Remove the cloves and cinnamon sticks before serving.

Yield: 4 to 6 servings

Taste the Flavor
ENTRÉES

Tobacco Road Food and Flavor Revitalization

Collard greens, fried okra, and barbecue.

No longer known simply for its tobacco presence and intense athletic rivalries, Durham and its surrounding areas are quickly becoming known for the unique farm-to-table food scene. With a passionate mixture of chefs, farms, baristas, brewers, and bakers, Durham and Chapel Hill have transformed what was a thriving tobacco region into one of the hottest food destinations in the South.

In recent years, both Durham and neighboring Chapel Hill have made *Bon Appétit* magazine's *Foodiest Small Towns in the South* list, as well as being featured in publications such as *Martha Stewart Living, Garden & Gun*, and *Southern Living*. Whether the food is being served in a quaint building downtown or being passed through the window of a food truck, one thing is certain—this cuisine has given locals another thing to be passionate about besides sports rivalries.

Where does this originate? Between the two areas, there are over 120 small farms within a fifty-mile radius, and more than ten Farmer's Markets are open weekly. Luckily, the Triangle is home to extremely talented chefs, including several James Beard award winners, to prepare this delicious fresh produce.

Durham's food scene has actually revitalized the downtown area by attracting new restaurants, coffee shops, and bars, and creating change in the way people eat in the Triangle. They care about where their food comes from, who is growing it, and, most importantly, that it is delicious.

Battle of Cane Creek Filet Mignon

BATTLE OF CANE CREEK

The Revolutionary War Battle of Cane Creek took place on September 13, 1781, in Orange County. Although the winner was indecisive, the four-hour battle inspired the Patriots, who went on to secure a major victory at the Battle of Kings Mountain one month later. It is said that following that battle, the triumphant Patriots feasted on a meal of beef and fresh produce gathered from the surrounding land. We hope that strawberries and goat cheese were included in that victorious steak meal!

2 (6-ounce) filet mignon steaks, wrapped in bacon
Cavender's Greek seasoning or other seasoning to taste
1 cup balsamic vinegar
2 tablespoons sugar or honey
12 strawberries, diced
4 ounces goat cheese
1/2 teaspoon black pepper
1 tablespoon unsalted butter
Whole strawberries for garnish

Rinse the steaks and pat dry. Sprinkle with the Greek Seasoning. Cook the balsamic vinegar and sugar in a small saucepan until the sugar is dissolved. Add the diced strawberries. Cook over medium heat until the sauce is thickened, stirring frequently. Coat the goat cheese with pepper; crumble. Sear the steaks in the butter in an ovenproof skillet to the desired degree of doneness. Sprinkle with the peppered goat cheese. Broil for 1 minute. Serve with the sauce. Garnish with whole strawberries.

Yield: 2 servings

Beef Tenderloin

1 (4- to 5-pound) beef tenderloin
1 egg, beaten
1 tablespoon celery salt
1 tablespoon onion salt

3/4 teaspoon paprika
1/4 teaspoon black pepper
1/4 teaspoon cayenne pepper

Trim the tenderloin to remove any silver skin or excess fat. Brush the tenderloin with the egg. Sprinkle with a mixture of the celery salt, onion salt, paprika, black pepper and cayenne pepper. Place on a rack in a roasting pan. Roast at 500 degrees for exactly 25 minutes for medium-rare; do not open the oven door. Let the roast rest for 5 to 10 minutes. Cut into steak-size slices.

Yield: 6 to 8 servings

Goat Cheese-Stuffed Meatloaf

1 1/2 pounds ground beef
1/2 cup breadcrumbs
Minced garlic to taste
Recaíto to taste
2 teaspoons chili powder
1/2 teaspoon salt

1/2 teaspoon pepper
2 handfuls fresh spinach leaves
8 ounces goat cheese, crumbled
1 (8-ounce) can tomato sauce
3/4 cup lightly packed brown sugar
1 teaspoon stone-ground mustard

Combine the ground beef, breadcrumbs, garlic, recaíto, chili powder, salt and pepper in a large bowl; mix well. Spread over a large piece of plastic wrap on a baking sheet and flatten into a 1/8-inch-thick rectangle. Layer the spinach evenly over the ground beef mixture. Sprinkle the goat cheese evenly over the spinach. Fold 1 long edge inward. Roll up using the plastic wrap, peeling wrap away as the loaf is rolled. The filling should be tightly contained within the roll. Pinch the ends together and smooth evenly to seal. Place on a wire rack on a baking sheet lined with foil. Combine the tomato sauce, brown sugar and mustard in a small bowl; mix well. Spoon half the sauce evenly over the top of the loaf. Bake at 350 degrees for 1 hour or until the meatloaf is cooked through. Cut into slices. Heat the remaining sauce over very low heat. Serve over the meatloaf.

Yield: 6 to 8 servings

Santa Fe Chili

What fall football game in Tobacco Road isn't complete without a slow cooker of chili at the tailgate party? Current UNC head football coach Larry Fedora, his wife, Christi, and family wouldn't dream of having a tailgate party without this chili. It is a tradition and is the coach's favorite as soon as the weather turns colder each season!

1 pound ground beef
1 package taco seasoning mix
1 envelope ranch seasoning mix
2 (16-ounce) cans pinto beans, rinsed and drained
1 (16-ounce) can black beans, rinsed and drained
1 (16-ounce) can red kidney beans, rinsed and drained
2 (16-ounce) cans whole kernel corn, drained
2 (8-ounce) cans seasoned diced tomatoes

Cook the ground beef in a large stockpot over medium heat until browned and crumbly, stirring frequently. Stir in the taco seasoning mix and ranch seasoning mix. Add the pinto beans, black beans, kidney beans, corn and tomatoes. Simmer for 30 minutes to 1 hour or until of the desired consistency, stirring frequently. Serve with cornbread.

Yield: 8 servings

Mad Hatter's Root Beer–Braised Lamb Shanks

4 lamb shanks
Salt and pepper to taste
2 tablespoons vegetable oil
1 cup diced onion
1/2 cup diced celery
1/2 cup diced carrot
2 cups (1×1-inch) turnip or rutabaga cubes
48 ounces high quality root beer
2 teaspoons chopped garlic
1 teaspoons chopped fresh thyme
1 teaspoon chopped fresh rosemary
Coarsely chopped chives or arugula for garnish

Season the lamb liberally with salt and pepper. Sear on all sides in the oil in a large pot over high heat. Add the onion, celery, carrot and turnips. Sauté until the vegetables are lightly browned; reduce the heat. Add the root beer, garlic, thyme and rosemary. Simmer for 4 hours or until the lamb can be cut with a spoon. Remove the lamb carefully to a plate. Cook the vegetables and sauce over high heat until the sauce is slightly thickened. Spoon the vegetables and sauce onto a large serving platter. Arrange the lamb shanks over the vegetables. Spoon a small amount of the sauce over the lamb. Garnish with chives.

Yield: 4 servings

MAD HATTER BAKESHOP & CAFE

This unique twist on lamb comes from the culinary geniuses at the Mad Hatter Bakeshop & Cafe in Durham, where you're always welcome to linger for a while. Treat yourself to fresh, locally sourced food, classic recipes, and unpredictable combinations that invite you to slow down and savor. Share a plate, a piece of cake, and some satisfying conversation with friends. The bakeshop at Mad Hatter offers a variety of sweets, but their real specialty is custom cakes. Any design can be crafted into a themed house-made cake just for you. The cafe offers breakfast, lunch, dinner, and weekend brunch as well as local beer and wine!

Party Pork Tenderloin

LAVENDER BOURBON SMASH

4 ounces fresh ginger
3 tablespoons dried lavender
1/2 cup brown sugar
1/2 cup filtered water
2 sprigs of fresh mint
4 ounces bourbon (or more depending on stress level)
Ice
3 ounces sparkling water
Sprigs of fresh mint for garnish

Peel and chop the fresh ginger. Combine the ginger, lavender, brown sugar and filtered water in a small saucepan and mix well. Bring to a boil. Remove from the heat and let stand to cool for 1 hour. Strain and store in an airtight jar in the refrigerator for up to 1 month.

Muddle 1 tablespoon of the ginger syrup with the mint. Add the bourbon and ice and shake to mix. Pour sparkling water to the top of the glass. Garnish with fresh mint.

1 (1 1/2- to 2-pound) pork tenderloin
1 1/2 cups vegetable oil
1/3 cup fresh lemon juice
1/2 cup white wine vinegar
3/4 cup soy sauce
2 tablespoons dry mustard
1 tablespoon black pepper
1 1/2 teaspoons minced fresh parsley
1 clove of garlic, crushed

Place the pork tenderloin in a glass dish. Combine the oil, lemon juice, vinegar, soy sauce, dry mustard, pepper, parsley and garlic in a large bowl; mix well. Pour over the tenderloin. Chill, covered, for 24 hours. Drain, reserving the marinade. Place the tenderloin on a rack in a broiler pan. Roast at 350 degrees for 30 to 45 minutes or to 165 degrees on a meat thermometer inserted into the thickest part of the tenderloin, basting frequently with the marinade. May be cooked on a grill.

NOTE: Serve with steamed green beans and fettuccine.

Yield: 4 servings

Margarita Pork Tenderloin

3 cloves of garlic, minced
1 green onion, minced
1/2 jalapeño pepper, minced
5 tablespoons minced cilantro
4 tablespoons tequila
2 tablespoons orange juice
3/4 teaspoon lime juice
1 teaspoon salt
1 teaspoon ground cumin
1/2 teaspoon chili powder
1 (1 1/2-pound) pork tenderloin

Combine the garlic, green onion, jalapeño, cilantro, tequila, orange juice, lime juice, salt, cumin and chili powder in a resealable plastic bag; mix well. Trim the pork tenderloin. Add to the marinade and seal the bag. Marinate overnight. Remove the pork tenderloin and place on a foil-lined baking sheet. Bake at 400 degrees for 30 minutes or to 137 degrees on a meat thermometer inserted into the thickest part of the tenderloin. Let rest, covered with foil, for 10 minutes. Slice on the diagonal to serve. The thickest part of the tenderloin may still be pink.

Yield: 6 servings

Krupnikas-Braised Pork Tacos

3 pounds country-style boneless pork ribs, cut into halves,
    or 1 pork butt or pork shoulder
2 teaspoons salt
Pepper to taste
Canola, coconut or vegetable oil
2 onions, cut into 1-inch cubes
1/2 bunch of celery, cut into 1-inch pieces
10 whole black peppercorns,
    or 1 tablespoon ground black pepper
2 bay leaves
2 cups Krupnikas or honey-spiced liqueur
8 cups brewed tea
1/2 bunch of fresh thyme

Season the pork with the salt and pepper to taste. Heat a large stockpot with enough oil to cover the bottom until the oil is very hot. Add the pork and cook until browned. Remove the pork. Reduce the heat to medium-high. Add the onions, celery, peppercorns and bay leaves. Cook until the onions are caramelized, stirring frequently. Add the Krupnikas, tea and thyme, stirring to deglaze the stockpot. Place the pork and Krupnikas mixture in a large roasting pan and cover with foil. Bake at 250 degrees for 4 hours or until fork tender. Remove the pork from the liquid. Strain and reserve the liquid. Shred the pork, adding a small amount of the liquid until of the desired consistency. Serve with homemade corn tortillas, pan-fried red, yellow and orange peppers, chopped garden-fresh tomatoes and chopped garden-fresh cilantro.

NOTE: Krupnikas is a locally produced spirit: a North Carolina wildflower honey–spiced liqueur made right here in Durham.

Yield: 6 to 8 servings

Butternut Pasta with Italian Sausage and Baby Spinach

1 pound butternut squash, peeled, diced
10 ounces pasta
12 ounces mild or spicy ground Italian sausage
1 tablespoon butter
1/4 cup chopped shallots
3 cloves of garlic, minced
Kosher salt and freshly ground pepper to taste
2 cups baby spinach, chopped
4 sage leaves, sliced (optional)
2 tablespoons freshly grated Parmesan cheese

Bring a large pot of salted water to a boil. Add the squash. Cook until the squash is tender. Remove to a blender using a slotted spoon and process until puréed. Add the pasta to the boiling water. Cook according to the package directions; drain, reserving 1 cup of the cooking water. Sauté the sausage in a nonstick skillet until browned and crumbly. Remove the sausage using a slotted spoon and drain the skillet. Melt the butter in the skillet over medium-low heat. Add the shallots and garlic. Sauté until tender and golden brown. Add the puréed squash to the skillet; season with salt and pepper. Stir in the reserved cooking water. Add the spinach, sage and cheese. Add the pasta and sausage and stir to coat the pasta with the sauce.

Yield: 6 servings

Almond Basil Pesto Chicken Bake

2 1/2 cups chopped cooked chicken
2 (10-ounce) cans cream of chicken soup
1 (16-ounce) package bowtie pasta,
   cooked and drained
1 (12-ounce) jar marinated artichoke hearts,
   drained and chopped
1 cup freshly grated Parmesan cheese
7 ounces Almond Basil Pesto (see sidebar)
1 (4-ounce) jar diced pimentos
1 cup oil-pack sun-dried tomatoes, cut into strips

Combine the chicken, soup, pasta, artichoke hearts, cheese, Almond Basil Pesto, pimentos and sun-dried tomatoes in a bowl; mix well. Spoon into a lightly greased 3 1/2-quart baking dish. Sprinkle with additional cheese if desired. Bake at 350 degrees for 35 to 45 minutes or until hot and bubbly.

Yield: 6 to 8 servings

ALMOND BASIL PESTO

Almond Basil Pesto incorporates into the Chicken Bake beautifully. It can also be served as a dipping sauce. Combine 4 cups fresh basil leaves, 1/2 cup dry-roasted almonds, 6 cloves of garlic, and 1 1/2 teaspoons kosher salt in a food processor. Process until the ingredients are finely chopped. Drizzle in 3/4 cup extra-virgin olive oil gradually, pulsing until mixed. Spoon into resealable plastic freezer bags. Store in the freezer for up to 1 month.

Carolina Fried Chicken

It shouldn't come as a shock that when sourcing our League for Fried Chicken and Sweet Tea recipes, they came pouring in. We've taken the best parts of all the League members' recipes and combined them into the perfect pair. Amen!

1/2 cup buttermilk
3 eggs
1 teaspoon vanilla extract
2 cups all-purpose flour
1 teaspoon salt
1 tablespoon black pepper
1 tablespoon cayenne pepper
1 teaspoon smoked paprika
1 teaspoon onion powder
1 teaspoon ground dried rosemary
3 boneless skinless chicken breasts
Corn oil for deep-frying
Salt and black pepper to taste

Whisk the buttermilk, eggs and vanilla in a small bowl. Combine the flour, 1 teaspoon salt, 1 tablespoon black pepper, cayenne pepper, paprika, onion powder and rosemary in a large bowl. Drizzle 2 tablespoons of the buttermilk mixture into the flour mixture, mixing until small clumps form. Spoon into a large resealable plastic bag. Dip the chicken into the buttermilk mixture. Place in the plastic bag and shake to coat. Place the chicken on a wire rack. Let stand for 10 minutes. Fill a cast-iron skillet or Dutch oven half full with corn oil and heat to 350 to 375 degrees. Fry the chicken in the hot oil for 10 minutes or until golden brown and to 160 degrees on a meat thermometer inserted into the thickest part of the chicken. Maintain the oil at 300 to 325 degrees while frying the chicken. Drain on paper towels. Season with salt and black pepper to taste. Serve warm.

Yield: 3 to 6 servings

SWEET CITRUS TEA

4 family-size tea bags
3 1/2 quarts filtered water
1 cup turbinado sugar
1/2 cup agave nectar
2 cups orange juice
1/2 cup fresh lemon juice
Orange slices

Steep tea bags in 1 quart of very hot water in a gallon pitcher. Combine 1 quart water and turbinado sugar in a saucepan and cook over high heat until the sugar is dissolved, stirring frequently. Stir in the agave nectar. Pour over the tea in the pitcher. Steep for 15 minutes. Remove the tea bags. Add the orange juice and lemon juice and remaining water to make 1 gallon. Stir in orange slices. Pour into ice-filled glasses.

Slow-Cooking Pulled Chicken

1 cup tomato sauce
1/2 cup ketchup
8 teaspoons brown sugar
8 teaspoons apple cider vinegar

2 teaspoons garlic powder
Red pepper flakes to taste
1 1/2 pounds boneless skinless
   chicken breasts

Combine the tomato sauce, ketchup, brown sugar, vinegar, garlic powder and red pepper flakes in a slow cooker; mix well. Add the chicken, turning to coat with the sauce. Cook, covered, on High for 3 to 4 hours or on Low for 7 to 8 hours or until the chicken is fully cooked. Remove the chicken to a cutting board and shred using 2 forks. Return to the sauce in the slow cooker; mix well.

Yield: 6 servings

Spicy Ginger Chicken Thighs

1 tablespoon coconut oil
6 boneless skinless chicken thighs
Sea salt and black pepper to taste
1 small white onion, diced
4 cloves of garlic, minced or grated

2 tablespoons freshly grated ginger
2 tablespoons white sesame seeds (optional)
1 or 2 pinches of chili flakes
1/2 cup soy sauce
1/4 cup rice vinegar

Heat the coconut oil in a cast-iron skillet. Season the chicken with sea salt and pepper. Place top side down in the skillet. Cook for 5 to 6 minutes or until the chicken is browned. Combine the onion, garlic, ginger, sesame seeds, chili flakes, soy sauce and vinegar in a small bowl; mix well. Turn the chicken over. Spread the sauce evenly over the chicken. Transfer the skillet to the oven. Bake at 425 degrees for 20 to 25 minutes or until the chicken tests done.

Yield: 6 servings

Brazilian Chicken

This recipe comes from Duke men's soccer coach John Kerr. It's a Kerr family favorite since they are huge fans of Brazilian soccer. Coach Kerr's father played soccer with the Great Pelé and has fond memories of the beautiful passing, creative dribbling, and ball control of the Brazil team. As a tribute, the Kerrs serve this recipe when hosting all of their soccer friends and guests.

1 medium onion, chopped
1 bunch of scallions, trimmed and
   chopped
1/2 cup trimmed cilantro
6 cloves of garlic
2 bay leaves

1 teaspoon salt
1 teaspoon pepper
1/2 cup dry white wine
1/2 cup olive oil
2 or 3 packages thin-sliced
   chicken breasts

Combine the onion, scallions, cilantro, garlic, bay leaves, salt, pepper, wine and olive oil in a food processor. Pulse until coarsely puréed. Coat the chicken with the mixture and place in a resealable plastic bag. Place the bag in a bowl and marinate in the refrigerator for 4 hours to overnight. Grill over hot coals until cooked through.

Yield: 8 servings

Camby Chicken

This recipe comes from Jenny Levy, head coach of women's lacrosse at the University of North Carolina at Chapel Hill. She serves her Camby Chicken with rice and green beans, and even picky eaters leave the table happy.

3 or 4 boneless skinless chicken breasts
6 tablespoons butter, melted
1/4 cup honey

1 tablespoon yellow mustard
1 teaspoon curry powder

Arrange the chicken in a greased baking dish. Bake at 350 degrees for 45 minutes. Combine the butter, honey, mustard and curry powder in a small bowl; mix well. Pour over the chicken breasts. Bake for 15 minute longer or until the sauce is hot and bubbly.

Yield: 3 or 4 servings

Chang and Eng's Chicken

1/2 cup basmati or jasmine rice
2 tablespoons butter
4 boneless skinless chicken breasts, cut into
   cubes
1 cup cornstarch
5 tablespoons olive oil
Juice of 1 lime
6 cloves of garlic, minced
1 to 2 tablespoons olive oil
Brussels sprouts to taste, cut into quarters
Broccoli florets to taste
1/3 cup cranberry juice

1/3 cup orange juice
1/3 cup peach juice, or juice of 1 peach
2 tablespoons rice vinegar
3 tablespoons tamari or soy sauce
1/4 cup turbinado or light brown sugar
2 tablespoons (or more) Sriracha sauce
1 tablespoon cornstarch
2 tablespoons water
3 or 4 cloves of garlic, minced
1 tablespoon olive oil
Chopped scallions, lime slices and peach
   slices for garnish

Prepare the rice according to the package directions. Stir in the butter. Keep the rice warm. Coat the chicken with 1 cup cornstarch. Sauté in 5 tablespoons olive oil in a large skillet over medium heat until cooked through and golden brown. Drain on a paper towel-lined plate. Sprinkle with the lime juice. Sauté 6 cloves of garlic in 1 to 2 tablespoons olive oil in a sauté pan until fragrant. Add the Brussels sprouts and broccoli. Cook, covered, over medium heat until tender-crisp.

Combine the cranberry juice, orange juice, peach juice, vinegar, tamari, turbinado sugar and Sriracha sauce in a bowl; whisk lightly. Whisk in 1 tablespoon cornstarch and water. Sauté 3 or 4 cloves of garlic in 1 tablespoon olive oil in a large skillet for 1 minute. Add the juice mixture. Bring to a boil, stirring constantly. Add the chicken. Cook for 1 to 2 minutes or until the sauce is slightly thickened. Layer the rice, vegetables and chicken on serving plates. Garnish with scallions, lime slices and peach slices. Serve with additional Sriracha sauce for the spice lovers at your table.

Yield: 6 servings

Saladelia's Chicken Apple Couscous

6 boneless skinless chicken breasts
Kosher salt, black pepper, ground cumin
    and dried thyme to taste
2 cups couscous
1/3 cup dried cranberries
1/3 cup raisins
1/4 cup chopped cilantro
1/4 cup dried apricots, cut into 1/4-inch cubes
2 cloves of garlic, finely shaved
2 tablespoons olive oil
2 teaspoons curry powder
1/2 teaspoon black pepper
4 cups chicken broth
1 Granny Smith apple, cored and cut into 1/4-inch cubes
Fresh cilantro for garnish

Season the chicken with salt, pepper, cumin and thyme to taste. Sear in a skillet. Bake at 450 degrees for 12 minutes or to 160 degrees on a meat thermometer. Let stand for 5 minutes. Meanwhile, combine the couscous, dried cranberries, raisins, cilantro and dried apricots in a large pot.

Sauté the garlic in the olive oil in a skillet over medium heat until translucent. Add the curry powder and 1/2 teaspoon pepper, toasting until aromatic. Add the broth and apple. Simmer over medium-high heat just until the apples are tender. Add to the couscous mixture. Let stand to cool. Cook for 10 minutes; remove from the heat. Slice the chicken across the grain. Fluff the couscous using a fork. Spoon the couscous mixture onto a serving platter. Top with the chicken. Garnish with fresh cilantro.

Yield: 6 servings

Glazed Chili Chicken

6 boneless skinless chicken thighs
2 teaspoons chili powder
2 teaspoons garlic powder
1 teaspoon paprika
1 teaspoon ground cumin

1 teaspoon salt
1/2 teaspoon cayenne pepper
1/4 cup apple cider vinegar
2 tablespoons honey

Coat the chicken in a mixture of the chili powder, garlic powder, paprika, cumin, salt and cayenne pepper. Arrange on a broiler pan. Broil on the top oven rack for 5 minutes per side. Whisk the vinegar and honey in a small bowl. Turn the chicken over. Baste with half the vinegar mixture and broil for 1 minute. Turn the chicken over. Baste with the remaining vinegar mixture and broil for 1 minute longer.

Yield: 6 servings

Chicken Piccata

3 boneless skinless chicken breasts
1 3/4 cups flour
2 tablespoons extra-virgin olive oil
Juice of 1 lemon
2 (8-ounce) cans chicken broth
1/4 cup (about) flour
1 (6- to 8-ounce) package sliced mushrooms

2 tablespoons extra-virgin olive oil
2 lemons, cut into slices
1 (3-ounce) jar capers
Salt and pepper to taste
1 (16-ounce) package angel hair pasta
Freshly grated Parmesan cheese to taste

Cut the chicken into small pieces. Coat with 1 3/4 cups flour. Brown in 2 tablespoons olive oil in a skillet. Sprinkle with the lemon juice. Add 1 1/2 to 2 cans of the broth. Stir in 1/4 cup flour to thicken. Sauté the mushrooms in 2 tablespoons olive oil in a skillet. Add to the chicken mixture. Arrange the lemon slices over the chicken. Cook, covered, over low heat until the chicken is cooked through; reduce the heat. Stir in the capers. Add additional flour to thicken the sauce if necessary. Season with salt and pepper. Prepare the angel hair pasta according to the package directions. Serve the chicken over the pasta. Sprinkle with Parmesan cheese.

NOTE: May serve over cooked white rice instead of pasta.

Yield: 4 servings

Lighter Chicken Parmesan

1/2 cup whole wheat flour
1/2 teaspoon salt
1/2 teaspoon black pepper
2 egg whites
1/2 cup skim milk
1 cup Italian breadcrumbs
4 thin-sliced chicken breasts
Nonstick cooking spray

1 (16-ounce) jar marinara sauce
1 cup shredded low-fat mozzarella cheese
  (optional)
2 tablespoons freshly grated Parmesan cheese
  (optional)
1 (16-ounce) package whole wheat spaghetti,
  cooked and drained

Mix the flour, salt and pepper in a shallow dish. Whisk the egg whites and milk in a second bowl. Place the breadcrumbs in a third bowl. Coat the chicken with the flour mixture, shaking off the excess. Dip in the milk mixture. Coat with the breadcrumbs, shaking off the excess. Arrange in a glass baking dish. Spray the chicken with the cooking spray for 5 seconds per side. Bake at 400 degrees for 15 minutes or until the chicken tests done and the coating is brown. Spoon the marinara sauce over the chicken; top with the cheeses. Bake for 10 minutes or until the cheese is melted. Serve over the hot spaghetti.

Yield: 4 servings

Parmesan Pecan Chicken

4 boneless skinless chicken breasts,
  pounded to 1/3 inch thick
2 cups buttermilk
2 cups pecan halves, ground
1 cup panko breadcrumbs

1/4 cup garlic powder
1 cup freshly grated Parmesan cheese
2/3 cup vegetable oil
Kosher salt and freshly ground black
  pepper to taste

Place the chicken in a shallow dish. Add the buttermilk, turning the chicken to coat. Chill, covered, for 1 hour or longer. Combine the pecans, panko, garlic powder and cheese in a shallow dish. Remove the chicken from the buttermilk. Coat evenly with the pecan mixture. Cook in the oil in a shallow skillet for 4 to 5 minutes per side or until golden brown. Drain on paper towels. Season with salt and pepper.

Yield: 4 servings

Dance Festival Favorite Chicken and Pasta Salad

6 ounces rotini
2 tablespoons sesame seeds
1/2 cup vegetable oil
1/3 cup soy sauce
1/3 cup white wine vinegar
2 tablespoons sugar
1/2 teaspoon salt
1/4 teaspoon pepper
3 cups chopped cooked chicken, chilled
1/2 cup chopped fresh parsley
1/2 cup thinly sliced green onions
8 cups lightly packed torn spinach leaves
Fresh sprouts or sliced mushrooms (optional)

Cook the pasta in a large pot of boiling salted water just until tender (al dente); drain. Rinse with cold water; drain. Place in a large bowl. Cook the sesame seeds in 1/4 cup of the oil over medium heat for 2 minutes or until golden brown. Cool. Combine the sesame seeds, remaining 1/4 cup oil, soy sauce, vinegar, sugar, salt and pepper in a bowl; mix well. Pour over the pasta. Add the chicken and toss gently. Chill, covered, for 8 hours or longer. Add the parsley, green onions, spinach and sprouts; toss lightly. Serve with crunchy breadsticks.

Yield: 8 servings

AMERICAN DANCE FESTIVAL

Each summer, the American Dance Festival (ADF) brings dancers, choreographers, and dance professionals from all over the country to celebrate modern dance in the heart of Durham. Called "one of the nations most important institutions" by *The New York Times*, ADF hosts modern dance schooling and performances at Duke University and the Durham Performing Arts Center to preserve, create, and showcase modern dance for all ages.

Skillet Rosemary Chicken

12 ounces small red potatoes
1 tablespoon fresh rosemary leaves
1 clove of garlic, smashed
1 teaspoon kosher salt
Pinch of red pepper flakes
1 lemon, cut into halves
2 tablespoons extra-virgin olive oil
4 boneless skinless chicken breasts
1 lemon, cut into halves
2 sprigs of fresh rosemary

Cook the potatoes in salted water to cover in a saucepan over medium-high heat for 8 minutes or until tender; drain. Combine the rosemary leaves, garlic, salt and red pepper flakes on a cutting board. Mince and mash into a paste using a large knife. Scoop into a bowl. Add the juice of 1 lemon and the olive oil, reserving the squeezed lemon halves; mix well. Add the chicken, turning to coat. Cook the chicken in a covered cast-iron skillet for 5 minutes or until brown; turn the chicken over. Add the potatoes. Drizzle with the juice of 1 lemon, reserving the squeezed lemon halves. Add the 2 sprigs of rosemary and 4 squeezed lemon halves. Roast at 450 degrees for 20 to 25 minutes or until the chicken is cooked through.

Yield: 4 servings

CAST-IRON SKILLETS

Unlike the nonstick skillets of today, cast-iron skillets require care, patience, and love. And the way they make your food taste is amazing. One of the oldest forms of cookware, cast-iron skillets heat evenly and are often passed down from generation to generation of family members. But don't go washing a cast-iron skillet with soap and water; in fact, don't wash it at all unless absolutely necessary. A thorough drying and rubbing with a little bit of vegetable oil, and it's clean and ready for whatever you're cooking next!

Nasi Goreng (Indonesian Fried Rice)

This recipe is a favorite of Anson Dorrance, head soccer coach of the Lady Tarheels at the University of North Carolina at Chapel Hill. He suggests serving it with steamed spinach for pregame perfection.

8 ounces boneless skinless chicken breasts,
   cut into bite-size pieces
Soy sauce for marinade
3 or 4 tablespoons vegetable oil or
   peanut oil
1/2 large sweet onion, chopped
1 clove of garlic, minced
8 ounces peeled deveined prawns
   or shrimp
3 or 4 green onions, chopped
1 to 2 teaspoons ground coriander

1 teaspoon ground cumin
Pinch of ground cardamom
Red pepper flakes to taste
2 to 3 cups cooked Japanese rice, chilled
3 tablespoons soy sauce
2 (heaping) tablespoons peanut butter,
   or more to taste
4 or 5 eggs, beaten and fried on both
   sides to resemble a thick pancake,
   cut into 1/2-inch squares

Marinate the chicken in soy sauce to cover for a few minutes. Heat the oil to 375 degrees in a wok or large skillet over medium-high heat. Add the sweet onion and garlic. Stir-fry for 3 to 5 minutes or until the onion is tender. Stir in the chicken, prawns, green onions, coriander, cumin, cardamom and red pepper flakes. Stir-fry for 5 minutes. Add the rice and 3 tablespoons soy sauce. Cook until heated through. Add the peanut butter a small amount at a time, mixing well after each addition. Cook for 3 to 5 minutes longer or until the prawns are pink and the chicken is cooked through. Stir in the eggs. Adjust the seasonings.

NOTE: May omit the prawns and/or substitute slivered pork roast for the chicken, or substitute chopped cooked bacon for the chicken and/or prawns.

Yield: 4 to 6 servings

Seared Chicken with Mango Avocado Salsa

MANGO AVOCADO SALSA

1 mango, peeled and diced
1 avocado, peeled and diced
1/4 cup finely chopped red onion
2 tablespoons chopped fresh cilantro
1 jalapeño pepper, seeded and finely chopped
Salt and pepper to taste

CHICKEN

2 teaspoons blackened seasoning
4 to 6 boneless skinless chicken breasts
1 teaspoon olive oil
1 lime, cut into halves

For the Mango Avocado Salsa, combine the mango, avocado, onion, cilantro, jalapeño, salt and pepper in a bowl and mix well.

For the Chicken, rub the blackened seasoning over the chicken. Sear in the olive oil in a skillet over high heat for 1 minute. Reduce the heat to medium. Cook for 3 minutes per side or until the chicken is cooked through. Remove to a serving plate. Squeeze the lime juice over the chicken. Top with the Mango Avocado Salsa.

Yield: 4 to 6 servings

CAROLINA COSMOS

These smooth Carolina Cosmos are a perfect pairing with the spicy chicken. Combine the freshly squeezed juice of 1 to 2 limes (about 1/2 ounce), 1 ounce Grey Goose vodka, 1/2 ounce triple sec, and 1/2 ounce cranberry juice in a martini shaker filled with crushed ice. Shake vigorously. Strain into a martini glass. Garnish the rim with a lime wedge.

Holiday Chicken Gumbo

1/2 cup butter
9 tablespoons all-purpose flour
3 cups hot water, or chicken or fish stock
4 chicken bouillon cubes
2 cups chopped celery
2 cups chopped green onions
1/2 cup chopped green bell pepper
4 tablespoons butter, or 2 to 3 tablespoons
   olive oil
2 to 3 cloves of garlic, minced
1 (15-ounce) can chopped tomatoes

1 bay leaf
1 to 2 tablespoons Worcestershire sauce
   or to taste
2 tablespoons Pickapeppa Sauce, or to taste
Cajun seasoning and/or cayenne pepper or
   black pepper to taste
2 to 3 cups chopped cooked chicken
12 to 16 ounces sliced cooked sausage
Hot cooked rice
1/2 cup chopped fresh parsley
1 tablespoon lemon juice

To make a roux, melt 1/2 cup butter in a heavy skillet or soup pot. Stir in the flour. Cook over medium heat for 20 to 30 minutes or until a rich brown color, stirring constantly. Add the water and bouillon cubes. Cook until the bouillon is dissolved, stirring constantly.

Sauté the celery, green onion and bell pepper in 4 tablespoons butter until tender. Add the garlic and sauté briefly. Add the tomatoes, bay leaf, Worcestershire sauce, Pickapeppa Sauce and Cajun seasoning; mix well. Combine the vegetable mixture and roux in a large stockpot. Bring to a boil; stirring frequently. Add the chicken. Simmer for 1 hour, stirring frequently. Turn off the heat. Let stand for 1 hour. Add the sausage. Reheat to serving temperature. Serve over rice. Sprinkle with parsley and drizzle with lemon juice.

NOTE: For a seafood version, substitute 1 pound white fish fillets with skin, such as amberjack or mahimahi, 1 small package crabmeat, 1 1/2 pounds shrimp, peeled, 1 small package oysters with liquid (optional) and 1 small package crab claws (optional) for the chicken and sausage. Return to a boil and simmer for 15 minutes.

Yield: 8 to 10 servings

Spaghetti Squash and Chicken Caprese Bake

1 large spaghetti squash, cut into
   halves and seeded
2 medium chicken breasts, baked
   and shredded
2 slices bacon, crisp-cooked and crumbled
2 cloves of garlic, minced
4 Roma tomatoes, coarsely chopped

1 (8-ounce) package sliced baby bella
   mushrooms
1 small handful fresh basil, coarsely chopped
1 cup fresh baby spinach, coarsely chopped
2 tablespoons extra-virgin olive oil
Salt and pepper to taste
1 cup mozzarella cheese

Place the squash cut side down on a baking sheet. Bake at 375 degrees for 35 minutes or until fork tender. Shred the pulp into "noodles" using a fork. Combine the squash noodles, chicken, bacon, garlic, tomatoes, mushrooms, basil, spinach, olive oil, salt, pepper, and 3/4 cup cheese in a large bowl; mix well. Spoon into a baking dish. Top with the remaining 1/4 cup cheese. Bake at 375 degrees for 45 minutes.

Yield: 4 servings

Duck Mignon

4 wild duck breasts, boned and cut into
   1/2-inch strips
2 cups apple juice (optional)
1 bottle low-sodium Worcestershire sauce
1 tablespoon Cavender's Greek
   seasoning

Juice of 4 lemons
1/2 cup packed light brown sugar
1/2 teaspoon salt
1 teaspoon pepper
3 cloves of garlic, minced (optional)
1 pound thinly sliced bacon

Marinate the duck in the apple juice in a large bowl overnight; drain. Remove the duck to a large resealable plastic bag. Add a mixture of the Worcestershire sauce, Greek seasoning, lemon juice, brown sugar, salt, pepper and garlic; seal. Marinate for 3 hours to overnight. Cut the bacon into halves. Wrap each slice around a bundle of 3 duck strips; secure with wooden picks. Grill over medium coals until the bacon is crisp.

Yield: 6 servings

Turkey Squares with Mushroom Gravy

TURKEY SQUARES
3 cups chopped cooked turkey
1 cup cooked rice or wild rice
2 cups soft breadcrumbs
1 rib of celery, diced
4 eggs, beaten
2 cups chicken broth
1 teaspoon salt
1/2 teaspoon poultry seasoning

MUSHROOM GRAVY
1 (4- to 8-ounce) can mushroom stems and pieces
2 tablespoons butter
1 tablespoon flour
3/4 to 1 cup milk

For the Turkey Squares, combine the turkey, rice, breadcrumbs and celery in a large bowl. Add a mixture of the eggs, broth, salt and poultry seasoning; mix well. Spoon into a greased 2-quart rectangular baking dish. Bake at 350 degrees for 1 hour or until set. Cut into squares.

For the Mushroom Gravy, sauté the mushrooms in the butter in a saucepan. Stir in the flour. Add the milk gradually, whisking until smooth. Cook until thickened, stirring constantly.

Top servings of the Turkey Squares with the Mushroom Gravy.

NOTE: May substitute chicken for the turkey.

Yield: 6 servings

Alivia's Durham Bistro's Herb-Crusted Salmon

1 (6-ounce) wild salmon fillet
2 ounces chopped fresh thyme
2 ounces chopped fresh parsley
2 ounces chopped fresh basil
2 ounces olive oil
3 tablespoons roasted garlic
4 asparagus spears, blanched and cut into pieces
3 ounces peas
2 tablespoons butter
White wine
5 ounces pappardelle (ribbon) pasta
1 tablespoon butter
Juice of 1 lemon

Sprinkle the salmon on both sides with a portion of a mixture of the thyme, parsley and basil. Sear the salmon flesh side down in the olive oil in an ovenproof sauté pan for 2 minutes per side, pushing the herbs into the fish using a spatula. Remove from the heat. Bake at 350 degrees for 5 minutes or until the internal temperature of the salmon reaches 350 degrees on a meat thermometer. Sauté the remaining herb mixture, garlic, asparagus and peas in 2 tablespoons butter in a sauté pan. Deglaze with the wine. Add the pasta, 1 tablespoon butter and lemon juice; mix lightly. Transfer to a serving plate. Top with the salmon.

Yield: 1 serving

ALIVIA'S DURHAM BISTRO

Alivia's Durham Bistro is located in the heart of Durham's Brightleaf Square, a location perfect for business lunches, pre-theater bites, and lounging on the outside patio. A restored bike shop, the restaurant's centerpiece is the 25-foot bar, which quickly became a favorite destination for both Duke and business crowds. This Herb-Crusted Salmon is pure Alivia's. With a focus on what's fresh, local, and popular in the South's trendiest food towns, it's not hard to see why Alivia's is a local favorite.

Teriyaki Salmon

1/4 cup maple syrup
2 tablespoons low-sodium soy sauce
Pinch of red pepper flakes

2 salmon fillets
1 1/2 tablespoons olive oil
Chopped chives for garnish

Combine the maple syrup, soy sauce and red pepper flakes in a small bowl. Marinate the salmon in half the mixture in a shallow bowl for 30 minutes per side. Heat the olive oil in a skillet over medium heat until hot but not smoking. Sear the salmon on 1 side; turn the salmon over. Sear the other side. Drizzle the remaining marinade over the top. Garnish with chives.

Yield: 2 servings

Grilled Halibut

4 halibut steaks
Salt and pepper to taste
4 tablespoons butter, melted
2 tablespoons white wine

2 tablespoons Dijon mustard
2 teaspoons dried tarragon
6 dashes of hot red pepper sauce, or to taste

Season the halibut with salt and pepper. Grill on oiled grill grates over medium to medium-high coals for 3 to 4 minutes per side or until the fish flakes easily, brushing liberally with a mixture of the butter, wine, mustard, tarragon and hot sauce.

Yield: 4 servings

Lobster Mac and Cheese

1 tablespoon vegetable oil
1 (16-ounce) package elbow macaroni
4 cups milk
6 tablespoons unsalted butter
1/2 cup all-purpose flour
12 ounces Gruyère cheese, grated (about 4 cups)
8 ounces extra-sharp Cheddar cheese, grated (about 2 cups)
1/2 teaspoon freshly ground black pepper
1 1/2 pounds cooked lobster meat
2 tablespoons butter
1 1/2 cups breadcrumbs

Bring a large pot of water to a boil. Drizzle with the oil. Add the macaroni. Cook according to the package directions for 6 to 8 minutes; drain well. Heat the milk in a small saucepan; do not boil. Melt 6 tablespoons butter in a large saucepan. Stir in the flour. Cook over low heat for 2 minutes, whisking frequently. Whisk in the hot milk. Cook for 1 to 2 minutes or until thickened, whisking constantly; remove from the heat. Stir in the Gruyère cheese, Cheddar cheese and pepper. Fold in the macaroni and lobster. Pour into a greased baking dish. Melt 2 tablespoons butter in a saucepan. Combine with the breadcrumbs, tossing to coat. Sprinkle over the macaroni. Bake at 375 degrees for 30 to 35 minutes or until bubbly and brown.

Yield: 6 to 8 servings

Lowcountry Boil

COCKTAIL SAUCE

1/2 cup ketchup
2 tablespoons prepared horseradish
5 dashes of Worcestershire sauce
Juice of 1 lemon
Hot red pepper sauce to taste

LOWCOUNTRY BOIL

1/4 cup Louisiana-style seasoning, such as
   Old Bay seasoning
4 pounds small red potatoes
2 pounds kielbasa or hot smoked link sausage,
   cut into 1 1/2-inch pieces
Brussels sprouts to taste (optional)
2 or 3 medium Vidalia or sweet onions,
   peeled and cut into quarters (optional)
6 ears of corn, cut into halves
Juice of 1 lemon
2 lemons, cut into halves
4 pounds large fresh shrimp, peeled and deveined
2 pounds crab legs (optional)
2 pounds crawfish (optional)
8 to 10 lobster tails (optional)

FROGMORE STEW OR LOWCOUNTRY BOIL?

Once called Frogmore Stew, this one-pot wonder was created by a National Guardsman when he needed to cook a meal for 100 soldiers. Richard Gay, who learned the recipe from his family, had everyone remembering his stew. The dish was later named Frogmore after Richard's home place. When the postal service eliminated the name, the popular dish was renamed Lowcountry Boil.

For the Cocktail Sauce, combine the ketchup, horseradish, Worcestershire sauce, lemon juice and hot sauce in a small bowl and mix well. Chill, covered, overnight.

For the Lowcountry Boil, fill a large pot with enough water to cover all the ingredients. Add the Louisiana-style seasoning and bring to a boil. Add the potatoes, sausage, Brussels sprouts and onions. Cook over medium heat for 20 minutes. Add the corn and cook for 10 minutes. Add the lemon juice, lemon halves and seafood. Cook for up to 3 minutes or until the seafood is cooked. Drain and turn out onto a newspaper-lined surface. Serve with the Cocktail Sauce, warm bread and melted butter.

Yield: 8 to 10 servings

The Carolina Inn's Shrimp and Grits

Nothing sounds as deliciously Southern as Shrimp and Grits. This scrumptious recipe is a timeless classic and an entrée that you will always find on the Inn's menu.

ANSON MILLS CREAMY GRITS
3 cups stone-ground grits
3 cups cold water
6 cups milk
1/2 cup butter
Salt and pepper to taste

COUNTRY HAM AND MADEIRA SHRIMP GRAVY
1 1/2 Vidalia onions, peeled, trimmed and julienned
3 tablespoons olive oil
4 ounces thinly sliced Virginia country ham, julienned
20 to 25 large shrimp, peeled and deveined
1 cup Madeira
Freshly ground pepper
2 cups heavy cream
1/2 cup chopped chives

THE CAROLINA INN

From casual get-togethers and intimate romantic dinners to quiet drinks, bar crawls, and pub ambiance, The Carolina Inn offers anything you're in the mood for when you're in Chapel Hill.

For the Anson Mills Creamy Grits, combine the grits with enough cold water to cover in a bowl. Let stand for a few minutes. Skim off any corn germ that floats to the top, stirring several times to remove as much corn germ as possible; drain. Combine 3 cups cold water and milk in a heavy saucepan. Bring to a simmer. Whisk in the grits to make a smooth mixture. Cook over low heat for 1 to 1 1/2 hours or until tender, stirring frequently. Add the butter, salt and pepper. If the grits become too thick, stir in a small amount of additional milk.

For the Country Ham and Madeira Shrimp Gravy, cook the onions in the olive oil in a heavy sauté pan until caramelized. Add the country ham. Cook for 45 seconds. Add the shrimp, tossing to mix. Add the Madeira and stir to deglaze the pan. Season with pepper. Cook until the Madeira is reduced by half, stirring frequently. Add the cream. Cook until reduced and thickened, stirring frequently. Stir in the chives. Spoon 4 ounces of the Anson Mills Creamy Grits onto each plate. Spoon equal portions of the Country Ham and Madeira Shrimp Gravy over the grits.

Yield: 6 servings

Easy Shrimp and Grits

This Shrimp and Grits recipe is perfect for a last-minute meal or easy weeknight meal. For an in-depth, elegant, classic recipe, see previous page. Serve either recipe with Southern Comfort Punch for a true Tobacco Road experience.

2 1/2 cups low-salt chicken broth
1 tablespoon butter
1 pound uncooked medium shrimp, peeled and shells reserved
3/4 cup quick-cooking white grits
3 tablespoons cream cheese, or fat-free cream cheese
2 tablespoons half-and-half, or fat-free half-and-half
1/2 cup chopped green onions
3 tablespoons butter
2 tablespoons fresh lime juice

Combine the broth and 1 tablespoon butter in a heavy medium saucepan. Bring to a boil. Add the shrimp shells. Cook until the shells turn pink; remove and discard the shells. Stir in the grits; reduce the heat. Simmer for 5 minutes, stirring occasionally. Add the cream cheese and half-and-half; mix well. Simmer, covered, for 7 minutes or until almost all the liquid has evaporated and the grits are tender, stirring frequently. Stir in the green onions; remove from the heat. Melt 3 tablespoons butter in a large heavy skillet over medium-high heat. Add the shrimp. Sauté for 3 minutes or just until the shrimp are cooked through. Stir in the lime juice. Spoon the grits onto serving plates. Top with shrimp and drizzle with the pan drippings.

Yield: 2 to 3 servings

SOUTHERN COMFORT PUNCH

Stir a fifth of Southern Comfort, 8 ounces lemon juice from concentrate, 6 ounces frozen lemonade concentrate, 6 ounces orange juice concentrate, 2/3 of a 2-liter bottle of lemon-lime soda, and 2/3 of a 2-liter bottle of ginger ale in a large pitcher. Serve over ice.

Picante Shrimp Pasta

12 ounces rigatoni
1/2 cup olive oil
1 1/2 pounds medium shrimp, peeled and
    deveined
1 green bell pepper, cored, seeded and cut
    into 2-inch strips
1 yellow bell pepper, cored, seeded and cut
    into 2-inch strips

1 cup sliced fresh mushrooms
1 tablespoon chopped fresh cilantro
2 teaspoons minced garlic
2 medium tomatoes, chopped
2 cups picante sauce
1/2 cup freshly grated Parmesan cheese

Cook the rigatoni according to the package directions just until tender; drain. Keep warm. Heat the olive oil over medium heat in a large skillet. Add the shrimp, green bell pepper, yellow bell pepper, mushrooms, cilantro and garlic. Stir-fry for 3 minutes or until the shrimp turn pink. Stir in the tomatoes and picante sauce. Simmer for 3 minutes. Spoon over the pasta in a serving bowl. Sprinkle with the Parmesan cheese. Serve immediately.

Yield: 4 servings

Maryland Crab Cakes

1 pound fresh lump crabmeat
1 egg
2 tablespoons horseradish mustard
2 tablespoons mayonnaise
1 tablespoon Old Bay seasoning

Hot red pepper sauce to taste
Salt and pepper to taste
1 sleeve saltine crackers, crushed
Canola oil for frying

Remove any shell pieces from the crabmeat. Combine the crabmeat, egg, mustard, mayonnaise, Old Bay seasoning, hot sauce, salt and pepper in a bowl; mix gently. Shape into 4 cakes. Roll in cracker crumbs, coating evenly on all sides. Arrange on a baking sheet. Chill for 20 minutes or longer. Fry in 1/2-inch of canola oil in a skillet over medium-high heat for 2 to 3 minutes per side or until golden brown and heated through. Serve with Cocktail Sauce (page 153) or tartar sauce.

Yield: 4 servings

Classic Baked Ziti

16 ounces ziti or penne
1 tablespoon salt
2 tablespoons olive oil
5 cloves of garlic, minced
1 (28-ounce) can tomato sauce
1 (14-ounce) can diced tomatoes
1 tablespoon dried basil
1 teaspoon sugar
1 teaspoon dried oregano
Salt and pepper to taste

16 ounces 1-percent cottage cheese
2 large eggs, lightly beaten
1 cup freshly grated Parmesan cheese
1 cup heavy cream
3/4 teaspoon cornstarch
8 ounces mozzarella cheese,
    cut into small cubes
1/2 cup freshly grated Parmesan cheese
Nonstick cooking spray

Add the ziti to 4 quarts boiling water and 1 tablespoon salt in a large pot. Cook for 7 to 9 minutes or just until tender; drain. Combine the olive oil and garlic in a large skillet. Cook over medium heat for 2 minutes, stirring frequently; do not brown. Add the tomato sauce, tomatoes, basil, sugar and oregano. Simmer for 10 minutes or until thickened; remove from the heat. Season with salt and pepper. Combine the cottage cheese, eggs and 1 cup Parmesan cheese in a small bowl; mix well. Combine the cream and cornstarch in a saucepan. Bring to a simmer over medium heat. Cook for 3 to 4 minutes or until thickened, stirring frequently; remove from the heat. Stir in the cottage cheese mixture, 1 cup of the tomato mixture and half the mozzarella. Add the pasta and stir gently to coat. Spoon into a 9×13-inch baking dish. Top with the remaining tomato mixture. Sprinkle with the remaining mozzarella and 1/2 cup Parmesan cheese. Cover with foil sprayed with nonstick cooking spray. Bake at 350 degrees for 30 minutes; remove the foil. Bake for 30 minutes longer or until the cheese begins to brown. Let stand for 10 minutes.

NOTE: To freeze the ziti, cover the unbaked casserole with 2 layers of foil and place in the freezer. Thaw in the refrigerator for 1 to 2 days. Increase the baking time to 1 hour and 15 minutes, removing the foil for the last 30 minutes. If baking while frozen, bake, covered with foil, for 11/2 hours. Uncover and bake for 30 minutes longer.

Yield: 8 servings

Brown Butter and Fried Sage Linguini

16 ounces linguini
Salt to taste
1/2 cup butter
8 to 10 sage leaves
2 tablespoons good-quality (Modena) balsamic vinegar
1/2 cup grated Parmigiano-Reggiano cheese

Add the linguini to 4 quarts boiling water and a liberal amount of salt in a large pot over high heat. Reduce the heat to medium-high. Cook just until tender; remove from the heat. Melt the butter in a shallow pan over medium-high heat. Cook until brown and bubbly, stirring frequently. Add the sage and vinegar; remove from the heat. Drain the pasta, reserving 1/3 of the cooking water. Add the pasta to the sage mixture. Stir in enough reserved pasta water to make of the desired consistency. Add the cheese, tossing to mix. Place in a serving bowl. Serve immediately.

Yield: 4 servings

BROWN BUTTER

Also known as beurre noisette (which literally translates as hazelnut butter), brown butter has all the great qualities of butter plus a nutty, toasted flavor that makes baked goods and sauces taste richer. And it is a pretty brown color. Solid butter is actually an emulsion of water and fat with a suspension of milk solids inside. By cooking the butter a tiny bit past its melting point, you can take the taste of your butter up a notch. Be sure to keep your eye on the butter when browning; it's easy to go from brown to burnt.

Summertime Spaghetti

TOMATOES IN SEASON

Nothings says summer better than a ripe, juicy local tomato. North Carolina ranks seventh in the nation in tomato production, growing more than one million pounds annually. Our tomato season runs from July to October. Heirloom varieties are becoming increasingly more popular since they tend to produce more interesting and flavorful crops. Seeds from the best varieties are saved and passed down from generation to generation. To be considered heirloom, the variety must have been available for fifty years.

2 pints cherry tomatoes, cut into halves, or
   6 small tomatoes, quartered
1/2 cup fresh basil, torn
1/4 cup loosely packed fresh parsley, coarsely chopped
1/3 cup olive oil
Kosher salt and pepper to taste
1 clove of garlic, finely chopped
1 (16-ounce) package thin spaghetti or penne
1/2 cup freshly grated Parmesan cheese, or 12 ounces
   small mozzarella cheese balls, quartered

Combine the tomatoes, basil, parsley, olive oil, salt, pepper and garlic in a large serving bowl. Marinate for 1 to 4 hours. Cook the spaghetti according to the package directions; do not overcook. Drain. Add the cheese to the serving bowl. Toss in the pasta; mix well. Enjoy!

Yield: 4 servings

Cavatappi with Spinach, Beans and Asiago Cheese

2 cups cavatappi
8 cups coarsely chopped fresh spinach
   leaves
2 cloves of garlic, chopped
2 teaspoons olive oil
1/2 cup shredded asiago cheese

1 (19-ounce) can cannellini beans,
   or other white beans, drained
2 tablespoons olive oil
1/4 teaspoon salt
1/4 teaspoon freshly ground pepper

Cook the cavatappi according to the package directions. Drain the cavatappi over the chopped spinach in a strainer to wilt the spinach. Sauté the garlic in 2 teaspoons olive oil in a small skillet. Combine the cavatappi, spinach, cheese, beans, garlic, 2 tablespoons olive oil, salt and pepper in a large serving bowl; toss to mix well. Sprinkle with additional pepper if desired.

Yield: 4 servings

Harvest Bowl

2 cups unsweetened coconut milk
1 cup water
1 1/2 cups rice
1 (16-ounce) can black beans
1 (16-ounce) can kidney beans

2 medium sweet potatoes, cut into
   bite-size cubes
1 teaspoon ground nutmeg
1/2 teaspoon sea salt
1 (10-ounce) can Mexicorn, drained
1/4 cup pineapple salsa

Combine the coconut milk and water in a large pot. Bring to a boil over high heat. Add the rice; reduce the heat to low. Cook, covered, for 25 minutes or until the water has evaporated. Combine the black beans and kidney beans in a small saucepan; cover. Cook over low heat for 20 to 25 minutes. Place the sweet potatoes in a large bowl. Microwave on Medium for 5 1/2 minutes or until tender. Sprinkle with nutmeg and salt. Layer the rice, sweet potatoes, drained beans, corn and salsa in a large bowl. Serve with hot sauce, additional salsa, cheese, sour cream and/or tortilla shells.

Yield: 4 to 5 servings

Four-Bean Chili

1 (28-ounce) can diced tomatoes
4 cups vegetable broth
1 (15-ounce) can black beans
1 (15-ounce) can cannellini beans
1 (15-ounce) can kidney beans
1 (12-ounce) can whole kernel corn
1 cup frozen baby lima beans
1 cup chopped onion
1 green or yellow bell pepper, seeded and chopped
2 cloves of garlic, minced
2 tablespoons chili powder
2 tablespoons dried oregano
2 teaspoons ground cumin
1 teaspoon ground coriander
1 to 2 teaspoons hot red pepper sauce (optional)
1/3 cup couscous
Salt and pepper to taste

Combine the tomatoes and broth in a slow cooker. Rinse and drain the black beans, cannellini beans, kidney beans and corn. Add to the tomato mixture. Stir in the lima beans, onion, bell pepper, garlic, chili powder, oregano, cumin, coriander and hot sauce; cover. Cook on Low for 6 to 8 hours or on High for 3 to 4 hours. Add the couscous. Cook, covered, for 10 minutes or until the couscous is tender. Season with salt and pepper. Serve with ½ cup shredded Mexican-blend cheese, 1/3 cup chopped fresh cilantro and sour cream.

Yield: 8 servings

Lentil-Stuffed Green Peppers

1 tablespoon olive oil
1 small or medium onion, diced
2 cloves of garlic, minced
1 medium carrot, finely chopped
1 small rib of celery, finely chopped
1 1/2 cups uncooked lentils
3/4 cup red wine
3/4 cup vegetable or chicken broth
1 (28-ounce) can chopped tomatoes
1 tablespoon chili powder
1 tablespoon ground cumin
1 tablespoon Worcestershire sauce
2 or 3 jalapeño peppers, diced (optional)
Salt and pepper to taste
8 medium to large green bell peppers,
    cut lengthwise into halves and seeded
2 cups shredded Cheddar cheese

Heat the olive oil in a soup pot over medium heat. Add the onion. Sauté until nearly translucent. Add the garlic, carrot and celery. Sauté for 4 to 5 minutes or until tender. Add the lentils, wine, broth, tomatoes, chili powder, cumin, Worcestershire sauce, jalapeños, salt and pepper. Simmer over medium heat for 15 to 20 minutes or until the lentils are tender and most of the water has been absorbed. Arrange the bell peppers on a parchment-lined baking sheet. Fill each halfway with the lentil mixture. Sprinkle with a small amount of the cheese. Fill with the remaining lentil mixture. Bake at 375 degrees for 25 minutes. Top with the remaining cheese. Bake for 5 minutes longer or until the cheese is melted.

Yield: 8 servings

LENTILS

Unlike other legumes, lentils cook quickly without presoaking, making them ideal for a healthy weeknight meal. Just make sure to rinse to remove any dirt or debris before cooking. To cook, add enough water (or broth for extra flavor) to cover the lentils. Bring the water to a rapid simmer over medium heat. Reduce the heat to a gentle simmer. Cook for 20 to 30 minutes or until tender. Taste the lentils during cooking to check for the appropriate consistency: firmer for a side dish or in a salad; softer if adding to a soup or stew.

Risotto with Roasted Sweet Potatoes and Spinach

3 large sweet potatoes, peeled and cut into bite-size cubes
2 tablespoons olive oil
Kosher salt and freshly ground pepper to taste
6 cups vegetable broth
2 shallots, minced
3 cloves of garlic, minced
4 tablespoons unsalted butter
1 1/2 cups Arborio rice
1/2 cup dry white wine
2 cups chopped fresh spinach
1 cup freshly grated Parmesan cheese

Spread the sweet potatoes on a baking sheet. Drizzle with the olive oil and toss to coat. Sprinkle with salt and pepper. Roast at 400 degrees for 25 to 30 minutes or until tender-crisp. Heat the broth in a saucepan; keep warm. Sauté the shallots and garlic in the butter in a Dutch oven over medium heat until lightly browned. Add the rice and stir to coat. Stir in the wine. Simmer for 2 to 3 minutes. Add the broth 1 cup at a time, stirring constantly until the broth is absorbed after each addition. Continue in this manner for 30 minutes or until all the broth is absorbed and the rice is creamy. Remove from the heat. Add the spinach, roasted sweet potatoes and cheese; stir gently to mix. Season with salt and pepper.

Yield: 4 servings

Butternut Squash Tart

CRUST

1 cup plus 2 tablespoons all-purpose flour
1/4 teaspoon kosher salt
1/4 teaspoon black pepper
1/4 teaspoon baking powder

1/4 cup extra-virgin olive oil
3 tablespoons ice water
Olive oil cooking spray

FILLING

3 cups cubed peeled butternut squash
3/4 cup chopped onion
1 tablespoon extra-virgin olive oil
1/2 cup Gruyère cheese
2 eggs
1/4 teaspoon kosher salt
1/4 teaspoon black pepper
4 ounces chopped pancetta

1 tablespoon extra-virgin olive oil
8 ounces sliced fresh gourmet blend
  mushrooms, such as baby bella, cremini,
  shiitake and oyster
1/4 teaspoon kosher salt
1/4 teaspoon black pepper
1/4 cup chicken broth
1/2 cup Gruyère cheese

For the Crust, combine the flour, salt, pepper and baking powder in a food processor. Pulse several times to mix. Whisk the olive oil and ice water in a small bowl. Add to the flour mixture through the food processor chute gradually, processing until crumbly. Sprinkle the mixture over the bottom of a 9-inch pie plate coated with olive oil cooking spray. Press evenly over the bottom and side of the pie plate. Bake at 425 degrees for 10 minutes.

For the Filling, place the squash in the food processor. Process for 1 minute or until finely chopped. Cook the squash and onion in 1 tablespoon olive oil in a large nonstick skillet over medium-high heat for 9 minutes, stirring occasionally. Combine 1/2 cup Gruyère cheese, eggs, 1/4 teaspoon salt and 1/4 teaspoon pepper in a bowl and mix well. Stir into the squash mixture. Spread evenly in the baked crust. Bake for 9 minutes. Cook the pancetta in 1 tablespoon olive oil in a skillet for 1 minute. Add the mushrooms. Cook for 7 minutes or until browned. Stir in 1/4 teaspoon salt and 1/4 teaspoon pepper. Add the broth. Cook for 1 minute or until the liquid evaporates. Spoon evenly over the squash mixture. Sprinkle with 1/2 cup Gruyère cheese. Bake for 3 to 5 minutes longer or until the cheese is melted.

Yield: 6 to 8 servings

Tomato Pie

CRUST
2 cups buttermilk baking mix
2/3 cup milk
1/3 cup flour
1 egg white
1 teaspoon water

FILLING
10 small tomatoes, or 3 large tomatoes, sliced
10 basil leaves (optional)
1 small onion, chopped
Salt and pepper to taste
2 cups shredded mozzarella cheese
1/2 cup freshly grated Parmesan cheese
1 cup mayonnaise or whipped salad dressing
1 cup breadcrumbs or crumbled Ritz crackers

For the Crust, combine the baking mix and milk in a small bowl; mix well. Roll out on a surface dusted with the flour. Fit into a deep-dish pie plate. Brush with a mixture of the egg white and water. Bake at 350 degrees for 30 minutes or until browned. Cool.

For the Filling, arrange the tomatoes in the baked shell, overlapping the slices. Sprinkle with the basil, onion, salt and pepper. Spread with a mixture of the mozzarella cheese, Parmesan cheese and mayonnaise. Sprinkle the breadcrumbs over the top. Bake at 350 degrees for 30 minutes or until lightly browned. Cool for 10 minutes before serving.

Yield: 6 servings

SOUTHERN HOSPITALITY

Southerners are known for being warm, gracious, friendly, and welcoming. We say please and thank you, open doors, make enough food to feed our neighbors, and we've never met a stranger. To the rest of the world, this combination of qualities is known as "Southern hospitality." But to Southerners, this is not a concept that needs a name or definition: it is just who we are, how we were raised, and our way of life.

ALL APPLES
+ PEARS 1.29 LB

Taste the Sweetness
DESSERTS

Tobacco Road Today

We've come a long way from the humble, yet noble, beginnings of Tobacco Road. The actual path between the "Big Four" schools that traditionally make up Tobacco Road widened from 46 miles to 105 miles when Wake Forest University moved to Winston-Salem, North Carolina. This increased distance also boasts more culture, community, and commerce than ever before.

Old Lucky Strike warehouses, which once filled downtown Durham with the sweet and distinctive smell of tobacco, now hold world-class sports, theater, research, education, and dining venues. An old farm just outside of Pittsboro has become one of the South's most celebrated restaurants. Remote farmland and forests now house Research Triangle Park—one of the most prominent high-tech research and development centers in the United States. Lunch carts have evolved into a bustling food-truck scene. What was once a small tobacco town is now a world-renowned medical center, and old tobacco fields are now host to renewable agricultural practices that are leading the country in sustainable food sources. Ancient Indian trading paths, which evolved into revolutionary war roads used during the battle for American Independence, now make up the famous nine miles of highway that connect the most historic rivalries in college sports and our beloved Tobacco Road.

Whether you are a veteran or novice of Durham and Orange Counties, now is the best time to discover why the South's Tastiest Town is also consistently named the "Best Place to Live and Work in the Country." It's an ever-changing scene where everything old is always new again, even better than before. This compilation of recipes and stories is our love letter to Tobacco Road. But don't take our word for it: get out there and discover it for yourself. It's so sweet!

Applesauce Cake

1/2 cup margarine, softened
1 cup sugar
1 cup cold applesauce
1 teaspoon baking soda
2 cups all-purpose flour

1 teaspoon ground cinnamon
1/2 teaspoon ground cloves
1/2 cup chopped nuts (optional)
1/2 cup raisins (optional)
Nonstick cooking spray

Cream the margarine and sugar in a large mixing bowl until light and fluffy. Add a mixture of the applesauce and baking soda; mix well. Combine the flour, cinnamon and cloves. Add to the batter, beating to mix. Stir in the nuts and raisins. Pour into a loaf pan sprayed with nonstick cooking spray. Bake at 350 degrees for 45 to 50 minutes or until the cake tests done.

NOTE: May bake in 8 cupcake cups sprayed with nonstick cooking spray. Bake at 400 degrees for 12 to 15 minutes or until the cupcakes test done.

Yield: 8 servings

Blueberry Lemon Bundt Cake

1 package butter-recipe yellow cake mix
1 (3-ounce) package lemon instant
   pudding mix
8 ounces cream cheese, softened

1/2 cup canola oil
3 eggs
2 cups fresh or frozen blueberries

Combine the cake mix and pudding mix in a large bowl. Cut in the cream cheese until crumbly. Add the canola oil and eggs and mix well. Fold in the blueberries gently. Pour into a greased and floured Bundt pan. Bake at 350 degrees for 45 minutes. Cover the top of the pan with foil. Bake for 15 minutes longer. Cool on a wire rack. Invert onto a cake plate.

Yield: 16 servings

Carrot Cake with Cream Cheese Frosting

CAKE

2 cups sugar

1 cup canola oil

3 eggs

2 cups all-purpose flour

2 teaspoons ground cinnamon

1 1/2 teaspoons baking soda

1/2 teaspoon salt

3 cups shredded peeled carrots

CREAM CHEESE FROSTING

16 ounces cream cheese, softened

1/2 cup butter, softened

1 teaspoon vanilla extract

1/4 teaspoon salt

1 1/2 pounds confectioners' sugar

For the Cake, combine the sugar and canola oil in a mixing bowl and beat until well mixed. Add the eggs, one at a time, beating well after each addition. Beat at medium speed for 2 minutes. Sift the flour, cinnamon, baking soda and salt together. Add to the batter gradually, beating well after each addition. Fold in the carrots. Pour the batter into two 9-inch cake pans lined with parchment paper. Bake at 350 degrees for 30 minutes or until the top springs back to the touch. Invert onto wire racks to cool. Remove the parchment paper.

For the Cream Cheese Frosting, combine the cream cheese and butter in a mixing bowl and beat until blended. Add the vanilla and salt; mix well. Sift in the confectioners' sugar a small amount at a time, beating constantly at low speed. Beat for 1 minute longer.

Spread the Cream Cheese Frosting between the layers and over the top and side of the cake.

NOTE: In a hurry? Make and bake the cake ahead of time and cool slightly. Wrap in plastic wrap and then in foil. Store in the freezer. Remove from the freezer and frost. Perfect for on-the-go entertaining.

Yield: 12 servings

Triple-Decker Strawberry Cake

CAKE

1 (18-ounce) package white cake mix
4 large eggs
1/2 cup sugar
1/2 cup finely chopped fresh strawberries

1 cup vegetable oil
1 (3-ounce) package strawberry gelatin
1/4 cup all-purpose flour
1/2 cup milk

STRAWBERRY ICING

1 cup butter, softened
32 ounces confectioners' sugar

1 cup finely chopped fresh strawberries

For the Cake, combine the cake mix, eggs, sugar, strawberries, oil, gelatin, flour and milk in a large mixing bowl. Beat at low speed just until blended; scrape down the sides. Beat at medium speed for 2 minutes. Pour into 3 greased and floured 9-inch round cake pans. Bake at 350 degrees for 23 minutes or until the cake springs back when lightly touched with a fork. Cool on wire racks for 10 minutes. Remove from the pans to cool completely.

For the Strawberry Icing, beat the butter in a mixing bowl at medium speed until light and fluffy. Add the confectioners' sugar and strawberries. Beat at low speed until creamy, adding additional confectioners' sugar if the icing is too thin or additional strawberries if the icing is too thick.

Spread the Strawberry Icing between the layers and over the top and side of the cake. Store in the refrigerator for up to 1 week or in the freezer for up to 6 months.

NOTE: If the icing pools at the bottom of the cake, chill for several minutes and respread using a wide spatula.

Yield: 12 servings

Chocolate Guinness Stout Cake

1/4 cup baking cocoa
1/3 cup Guinness draught stout
1 cup all-purpose flour
3/4 teaspoon baking soda
1/4 teaspoon baking powder
1/8 teaspoon salt
5 1/3 tablespoons butter, softened
1 cup sugar
2 large eggs
1/2 teaspoon vanilla extract
1/3 cup buttermilk
Chocolate Guinness Sauce (recipe on page 175)
Chocolate Ganache Glaze (recipe on page 175)

Combine the baking cocoa and stout in a small saucepan. Cook over medium-low heat until blended and smooth, stirring frequently; cool. Sift the flour, baking soda, baking powder and salt together. Cream the butter in a large mixing bowl. Add the sugar gradually, beating until pale yellow. Add the eggs, one at a time, beating well after each addition. Beat in the vanilla. Stir the buttermilk into the stout mixture. Add, 1/3 at a time, to the butter mixture alternately with the flour mixture, beginning with the stout mixture and ending with the flour mixture, beating on low after each addition. Batter will appear grainy. Pour into a greased and lightly floured 9-inch cake pan. Bake on the middle rack at 350 degrees for 25 to 35 minutes or until the cake pulls away from the sides of the pan and a wooden pick inserted in the center comes out clean. Cool in the pan on a wire rack for 10 minutes.

Place parchment or waxed paper under the wire rack. Invert the cake onto the wire rack; poke holes in the bottom of the cake using a fork. Spoon 3/4 of the Chocolate Guinness Sauce over the cake; let stand to allow the sauce to be absorbed. Invert the cake onto a cake plate; poke holes in the top of the cake. Spoon the remaining sauce over the cake. Pour the Chocolate Ganache Glaze over the cake, smoothing over the top and side. May pipe the remaining glaze in patterns over the cake or reserve for another use.

Yield: 8 to 10 servings

Chocolate Guinness Sauce

1/4 cup Guinness draught stout
1/4 cup packed light or dark brown sugar
2 tablespoons baking cocoa
1/2 teaspoon vanilla extract

Combine the stout, brown sugar, baking cocoa and vanilla in a small saucepan. Cook over low heat, stirring until smooth.

Chocolate Ganache Glaze

1 1/4 cups heavy whipping cream
10 ounces semisweet or dark chocolate chips,
   or dark chocolate bar, broken into pieces

Bring the cream to a simmer in a small saucepan; turn off the heat. Add the chocolate chips and stir until melted.

THE CRUNKLETON

If the name of the cake makes you thirsty for a beverage, consider popping into The Crunkleton in Chapel Hill. The Crunkleton is a uniquely modern establishment with the vintage feel of a bygone era. Visitors there can choose from over 500 distilled spirits, mixed with the same techniques and ingredients used decades ago. The Crunkleton also offers draft and bottled beers as well as wine by the glass and bottle.

Chocolate Pound Cake

1/2 pound butter, softened
1/2 cup shortening
3 cups sugar
2 teaspoons vanilla extract
5 eggs
3 cups all-purpose flour
1/2 cup baking cocoa
1 teaspoon salt
1/2 teaspoon baking powder
1 cup whole milk

Cream the butter, shortening and sugar in a large mixing bowl until light and fluffy. Add the vanilla. Add the eggs, one at a time, beating well after each addition. Sift the flour, baking cocoa, salt and baking powder together 2 times. Add to the butter mixture alternately with the milk, beating well after each addition. Pour into a greased 10-inch loaf pan. Bake at 300 degrees for 1 1/2 hours. Cool on a wire rack for 10 minutes before inverting onto a cake plate.

Yield: 10 to 12 servings

CHOCOLATE MARTINIS

There is nothing better than a chocolate martini! Mix together 1/2 shot Stoli Vanil Vodka, 1 shot Godiva Dark Chocolate Liqueur, and splashes of Frangelico Liqueur and Baileys Irish Cream. Pour over ice in a shaker and shake. Add a splash of heavy cream. Swirl chocolate syrup in a chilled martini glass. Strain the martini into the glass. Cheers!

Brown Sugar Pound Cake

1 pound butter, softened
1 cup sugar
2 cups packed brown sugar
6 eggs
4 cups all-purpose flour
3/4 cup milk
1 teaspoon lemon extract
1 teaspoon almond extract

Cream the butter, sugar and brown sugar in a large mixing bowl. Add the eggs, one at a time, beating well after each addition. Add the flour alternately with the milk, beating well after each addition. Add the lemon extract and almond extract; mix well. Pour into a greased and floured tube pan. Bake at 300 degrees for 1 hour and 40 minutes. Cool in the pan for 10 to 15 minutes. Invert onto a wire rack to cool completely.

Yield: 12 to 16 servings

LOCAL YOGURT

If you're looking for a sweet, frozen treat to accompany this cake, look no further than Local Yogurt, Durham's first independently owned frozen yogurt shop! Local Yogurt is both good and good for you. They are dedicated to enhancing the community by sourcing toppings from local farms and vendors and giving back to organizations active in our community. Local Yogurt can also help cater special occasions and events with the LoYo On The Go mobile unit.

Molten Chocolate Cakes

8 ounces bittersweet chocolate, chopped
1 cup unsalted butter
2 teaspoons vanilla extract
4 eggs

4 egg yolks
1/2 cup sugar
4 teaspoons all-purpose flour

Melt the chocolate and butter in a small saucepan, stirring until blended. Stir in the vanilla; cool. Beat the eggs, egg yolks and sugar in a mixing bowl until thick and pale. Add the chocolate mixture and flour. Beat just until mixed. Spoon into eight 4-ounce buttered and floured ramekins. Arrange on a baking sheet. Bake at 450 degrees for 10 minutes or until the sides are set and tops are puffed. Invert onto serving plates and serve immediately with good vanilla gelato.

Yield: 8 servings

Sweet Potato and Salted Vanilla Caramel Bacon Cupcakes

1 cup organic unsalted butter, melted
  and cooled
1 cup packed brown sugar
1 cup sugar
4 eggs, lightly beaten
2 cups organic all-purpose flour
2 teaspoons ground cinnamon
1 teaspoon baking powder

1 teaspoon baking soda
1 teaspoon salt
1/2 teaspoon ground ginger
1/4 teaspoon ground nutmeg
1 (15-ounce) can sweet potato purée
Salted Vanilla Caramel Sauce (recipe below)
8 ounces thin-sliced bacon, cooked and crumbled
Cream cheese frosting

Cream the butter, brown sugar and sugar in a large mixing bowl until light and fluffy. Add the eggs and beat well. Add a mixture of the flour, cinnamon, baking powder, baking soda, salt, ginger and nutmeg; mix well. Whisk in the sweet potato purée. Fill paper-lined cupcake cups 3/4 full. Bake at 350 degrees for 20 to 25 minutes or until golden brown and a wooden pick inserted in the centers comes out clean. Cool on a wire rack. Microwave a large spoonful of the Salted Vanilla Caramel Sauce in a glass bowl for 10 seconds. Add the bacon and toss to coat. Frost the cupcakes with cream cheese frosting. Sprinkle with the salted caramel bacon.

Yield: 1 dozen

Salted Vanilla Caramel Sauce

1 vanilla bean, sliced lengthwise into halves
1 cup heavy cream, at room temperature
2 cups sugar

1 1/2 sticks unsalted butter, cut into small pieces
  and softened
1 tablespoon kosher salt or smoked salt

Scrape the seeds out of the vanilla bean. Simmer the cream, vanilla bean seeds and vanilla bean pod in a small saucepan for 15 minutes; do not scald. Discard the vanilla bean pod. Cook the sugar in a saucepan over medium-high heat until amber, swirling frequently; remove from the heat. Add the butter, several pieces at a time, whisking briskly after each addition. Reheat for 30 seconds; remove from the heat. Add the cream mixture, whisking vigorously until the cream is incorporated. Add the salt, whisking until shiny and smooth. Cool for 15 minutes. Store in a glass jar.

Yield: 3 to 4 cups

Chocolate Cupcakes with The Best Peanut Butter Icing

CUPCAKES
3/4 cup butter, softened
2/3 cup sugar
1/2 cup packed brown sugar
2 eggs
1 cup buttermilk

1/2 cup low-fat sour cream
2 tablespoons brewed coffee
1 3/4 cups all-purpose flour
3/4 cup baking cocoa
1 1/2 teaspoons baking soda

THE BEST PEANUT BUTTER ICING
1 to 1 1/2 cups confectioners' sugar
1 cup creamy peanut butter
1/3 cup plus 1 teaspoon heavy cream

1 tablespoon butter
1/4 teaspoon vanilla extract

For the Cupcakes, cream the butter, sugar and brown sugar in a mixing bowl until light and fluffy. Add the eggs; mix well. Add a mixture of the buttermilk, sour cream and coffee; mix well. Sift the flour, baking cocoa and baking soda together. Add to the creamed mixture and mix until smooth. Spoon into paper-lined cupcake cups. Bake at 350 degrees for 25 minutes. Cool on a wire rack.

For The Best Peanut Butter Icing, combine the confectioners' sugar, peanut butter, cream, butter and vanilla in a mixing bowl; mix well. Add additional confectioners' sugar if necessary to make of spreading consistency.

Pipe The Best Peanut Butter Icing onto the cupcakes.

Yield: 1 dozen

Almond Cookies (Snowballs)

1/2 cup slivered almonds
1 cup butter, softened
1 cup confectioners' sugar
1 teaspoon vanilla extract

2 1/2 cups all-purpose flour
1/4 teaspoon salt
1/2 cup confectioners' sugar

Toast the almonds in a single layer in a shallow baking pan at 350 degrees for 6 minutes, stirring after 3 minutes. Let stand to cool for 20 minutes or until completely cooled. Reduce the oven temperature to 325 degrees. Process the almonds in a food processor for 30 seconds or until finely ground. Cream the butter in a mixing bowl. Add 1 cup confectioners' sugar and vanilla gradually, beating well after each addition; dough will be crumbly. Add a mixture of the flour, salt, and ground almonds gradually, beating until blended. Shape into 3/4-inch balls. Arrange 2 inches apart on parchment-lined cookie sheets. Bake for 12 to 15 minutes or until the edges are light brown. Cool for 2 minutes on the cookie sheet. Remove to wire racks. Cool for 10 minutes. Roll cookies in 1/2 cup confectioners' sugar to coat.

Yield: 6 dozen

Pretzel-Bottom Blondies

2 cups crushed pretzels
1/2 cup sugar
1/2 cup butter, melted
1 cup butter, softened
3/4 cup packed light brown sugar
1/2 cup sugar

2 eggs
2 teaspoons vanilla extract
2 1/4 cups white wheat or all-purpose flour
1 teaspoon baking soda
1 (8-ounce) package Reese's Peanut Butter
    Cups Minis

Combine the pretzels, 1/2 cup sugar and melted butter in a bowl; mix well. Press firmly over the bottom of a 9×13-inch baking dish. Bake at 350 degrees for 8 minutes. Cream the softened butter, brown sugar and 1/2 cup sugar in a mixing bowl until light and fluffy. Add the eggs and vanilla, beating until smooth. Add a mixture of the flour and baking soda gradually, beating until evenly mixed. Stir in the peanut butter cups, distributing evenly. Press over the baked pretzel crust. Bake for 30 minutes. Bake, covered, with foil, for 15 minutes longer. Cool completely on a wire rack until the center is firm. Cut into squares.

Yield: 2 dozen

Carolina Brewery's Double Chocolate Brownies

CAROLINA BREWERY

This decadent dessert is a staple at Carolina Brewery. Founded in Chapel Hill in 1995, Carolina Brewery is locally owned and has been serving contemporary American cuisine and award-winning handcrafted beer for over twenty years. Carolina Brewery uses fresh, in-season fruits and vegetables and locally raised beef on its menu, featuring both traditional and seasonal favorites. With two popular locations, award-winning beer, and a high-quality dining experience, Carolina Brewery is far from your typical brewpub.

6 large eggs
1 1/2 cups sugar
1 1/2 cups packed brown sugar
1 1/2 cups (12 ounces) butter, melted
1 1/2 cups baking cocoa
3/4 cup all-purpose flour
1 tablespoon vanilla extract
3/4 teaspooon kosher salt
1 (8-ounce) package semisweet chocolate chips

Beat the eggs using the whisk attachment in a mixing bowl until light and fluffy. Add the sugar and brown sugar gradually, beating until incorporated after each addition. Add the butter, cocoa, flour, vanilla and salt, mixing well after each addition. Stir in the chocolate chips. Spray a 9×12-inch baking pan with nonstick cooking spray. Line with parchment paper. Spray with nonstick cooking spray. Spoon the chocolate mixture into the prepared pan. Bake at 325 degrees for 40 minutes or until the brownies test done. Let stand for 1 hour. Chill until firm. Cut into 18 squares. Place in a container lined with parchment paper. Cover with an airtight lid and store in the refrigerator.

Yield: 18 brownies

Chocolate Cranberry Oatmeal Delights

1/3 cup all-purpose flour
1/3 cup whole wheat flour
1 1/2 cups old-fashioned oats
1 teaspoon baking soda
1/2 teaspoon salt
6 tablespoons unsalted butter, melted

3/4 cup packed light brown sugar
1 teaspoon vanilla extract
1 large egg, lightly beaten
1 cup dried cranberries
2/3 cup dark chocolate chips
Nonstick cooking spray

Combine the all-purpose flour, whole wheat flour, oats, baking soda and salt in a mixing bowl. Add a mixture of the butter and brown sugar. Beat at medium speed until blended. Add the vanilla and egg. Beat until blended. Fold in the dried cranberries and chocolate chips. Drop by tablespoonfuls 2 inches apart on cookie sheets sprayed with nonstick cooking spray or lined with parchment paper. Bake at 350 degrees for 12 minutes. Cool for 3 minutes or until the cookies are almost firm. Remove to wire racks to cool completely.

NOTE: Dried cherry-flavored cranberries may be substituted for the dried cranberries.

Yield: 4 dozen

Chocolate Marshmallow Bark

8 ounces Ghirardelli or other fine bittersweet chocolate
2 teaspoons butter
3 cups miniature marshmallows

Melt the chocolate and butter in a double boiler over medium heat, stirring occasionally. Remove from the heat. Stir in the marshmallows. Scrape into a 9 x 9-inch pan lined with heavy-duty aluminum foil using a silicone spatula, smoothing the surface. Chill for 1 hour or until the chocolate is set. Store in the refrigerator until serving time. Cut into pieces.

Yield: 1 dozen

Never-Fail Fudge

5 cups sugar
1 1/2 cups margarine
1 (12-ounce) can evaporated milk
6 ounces semisweet baking chocolate

12 ounces semisweet chocolate chips
1 jar marshmallow creme
1 teaspoon vanilla extract
2 cups chopped nuts (optional)

Combine the sugar, margarine and evaporated milk in a saucepan. Bring to a high rolling boil; reduce the heat just enough to still maintain a boil. Cook for 1 to 2 minutes longer, stirring constantly; remove from the heat. Melt the baking chocolate and chocolate chips in a double boiler. Fold the melted chocolate and marshmallow creme into the sugar mixture. Stir until the mixture is blended and thick. Stir in the vanilla and nuts. Pour into two well-greased 9 x 9-inch pans. Let stand until firm. Cut into squares.

Yield: 5 dozen

Chocolate Peanut Butter Bars

1 cup sugar
1 cup dark corn syrup
1 cup peanut butter

6 cups Special K cereal
6 ounces semisweet chocolate chips
6 ounces butterscotch chips

Combine the sugar and corn syrup in a 3-quart saucepan. Bring to a boil, stirring frequently. Remove from the heat. Add the peanut butter and stir until melted. Fold in the cereal. Spread in a 9 x 12-inch or 9 x 13-inch dish. Press the mixture using a piece of waxed paper; smooth the top. Melt the chocolate chips and butterscotch chips in a double boiler or in a microwave-safe dish. Spread over the cereal mixture. Chill for 20 minutes or just until slightly cooled. Cut immediately into squares.

NOTE: If using the microwave to melt the chocolate chips and butterscotch chips, place the chips in a microwave-safe bowl and melt at 70-percent power in 30-second bursts until the chips are almost melted, stirring between intervals.

Yield: 12 bars

White Chocolate–Topped Cinnamon Chip Bars

1/2 cup unsalted butter, melted and cooled
1 large egg
1 cup packed light brown sugar
1 tablespoon vanilla extract
1 tablespoon ground cinnamon

1 cup all-purpose flour
1 (10-ounce) package cinnamon chips
Nonstick cooking spray
8 ounces white candy melts, Vanilla CandiQuick or white chocolate candy bar

Combine the butter, egg, brown sugar, vanilla and cinnamon in a mixing bowl; mix well. Stir in the flour just until mixed; do not overmix. Stir in 1 1/4 cups of the cinnamon chips. Spoon into an 8 × 8-inch baking pan lined with foil sprayed with nonstick cooking spray. Smooth the top using a spatula. Bake at 350 degrees for 18 to 20 minutes or until a wooden pick inserted in the center comes out clean; cool. Melt the white chocolate according to the package directions. Spread over the baked layer. Sprinkle with the remaining cinnamon chips. Let stand until the white chocolate is firm. Cut into bars. Store in an airtight container for up to 1 week or in the freezer for up to 6 months.

NOTE: Do not overcook the white chocolate as it will scorch and seize up easily, and you will have to discard it and start over.

Yield: 32 bars

Forgotten Kisses

2 egg whites, at room temperature
1/4 teaspoon cream of tartar
1/8 teaspoon salt

2/3 cup sugar
6 ounces chocolate chips
1/2 cup ground pecans

Preheat the oven to 400 degrees. Beat the egg whites with the cream of tartar and salt in a large mixing bowl until stiff peaks form. Add the sugar gradually, beating at high speed until the meringue is very stiff and glossy. Fold in the chocolate chips and pecans. Drop by teaspoonfuls onto a well greased cookie sheet. Place in the oven; turn the oven off. Let stand in the unheated oven for 6 hours to overnight. Store in an airtight container.

Yield: 3 dozen

Vanilla Cream–Stuffed Chocolate Chip Cookies

COOKIES

1 cup plus 2 tablespoons all-purpose flour
1 teaspoon baking soda
1/3 teaspoon kosher salt
1 cup butter, softened

1/3 cup sugar
1/2 cup lightly packed brown sugar
1 egg
1 teaspoon vanilla extract

VANILLA CREAM

3 3/4 cups confectioners' sugar
1/2 cup butter, softened

1 teaspoon vanilla extract
1/4 cup heavy cream

GANACHE

1 cup semisweet chocolate chips
5 tablespoons heavy cream

2 1/2 tablespoons corn syrup

For the Cookies, mix the flour, baking soda and salt. Cream the butter, sugar and brown sugar in a mixing bowl until light and fluffy. Add the egg and vanilla and beat at low speed for 1 minute. Add the flour mixture. Beat for 2 minutes longer. Chill for 30 minutes.

For the Vanilla Cream, combine the confectioners' sugar, butter, vanilla and cream in a mixing bowl. Beat at high speed until light and fluffy.

Roll out the cookie dough 1/6 inch thick on a floured surface. Cut out using a round cookie cutter. Arrange half the rounds on a greased cookie sheet. Spoon 1 teaspoon of the Vanilla Cream onto the center of each round. Top with the remaining rounds, sealing the edges. Bake at 375 degrees for 12 minutes. Cool on a wire rack.

For the Ganache, place the chocolate chips in a metal bowl. Bring the cream and corn syrup to a simmer in a saucepan, stirring frequently. Pour over the chocolate chips and stir until the chocolate is melted.

Drizzle the Ganache over the cookies. Let stand to cool completely.

Yield: 2 dozen

Chai Tea Eggnog Cookies

4 chai tea bags
1 (17-ounce) package sugar cookie mix
1/2 cup butter, melted
1 large egg

2 tablespoons eggnog
1 cup confectioners' sugar
1/2 teaspoon freshly grated nutmeg
2 tablespoons eggnog

Remove the tea leaves from each tea bag. Combine with the cookie mix, butter, egg and 2 tablespoons eggnog in a bowl; mix well. Drop by tablespoonfuls onto parchment-lined cookie sheets. Bake at 350 degrees for 8 to 10 minutes or until lightly browned. Cool on a wire rack. Whisk the confectioners' sugar, nutmeg and 2 tablespoons eggnog in a small bowl until smooth. Pour over the cooled cookies.

NOTE: May use 2 packages sugar cookie mix, 1 cup butter, 1 egg and 2 tablespoons eggnog, baking and glazing as directed above.

Yield: 2 dozen

White Chocolate Macadamia Nut Cookies

1 cup butter, softened
3/4 cup packed light brown sugar
1/2 cup sugar
2 eggs
1/2 teaspoon vanilla extract
1/2 teaspoon almond extract

2 1/2 cups all-purpose flour
1 teaspoon baking soda
1/2 teaspoon salt
1 cup chopped macadamia nuts
1 cup white chocolate chips

Cream the butter, brown sugar and sugar in a mixing bowl until light and fluffy. Add the eggs, one at a time, beating well after each addition. Stir in the vanilla extract and almond extract. Add a mixture of the flour, baking soda and salt gradually, mixing well after each addition. Fold in the macadamia nuts and white chocolate chips. Drop by teaspoonfuls onto ungreased cookie sheets. Bake at 350 degrees for 10 minutes or until golden brown. Cool on the cookie sheets on a wire rack for 5 minutes. Remove the cookies to the wire rack to cool completely.

Yield: 3 dozen

Lemon Bars with Basil Whipped Cream

BASIL WHIPPED CREAM

2 cups heavy whipping cream
2 ounces fresh basil leaves

2 tablespoons sugar

BARS

Nonstick cooking spray
1 cup butter, softened
2 cups all-purpose flour
1 cup sugar
6 eggs

1 cup sugar
1 cup all-purpose flour
2/3 cup fresh lemon juice
Zest of 1 lemon
Confectioners' sugar

For the Basil Whipped Cream, combine the cream and basil in a saucepan. Simmer over low heat for 10 minutes; strain to remove the basil. Chill the cream in a mixing bowl overnight.

For the Bars, line a 9×13-inch baking pan with foil sprayed with nonstick cooking spray. Combine the butter, 2 cups flour and 1 cup sugar in a mixing bowl; mix well. Press over the bottom of the prepared pan. Bake at 350 degrees for 15 minutes. Beat the eggs and 1 cup sugar in a mixing bowl until light and fluffy. Add 1 cup flour gradually, beating constantly. Beat in the lemon juice and lemon zest. Pour over the baked crust. Bake for 20 to 30 minutes or until set. Let stand to cool. Chill for several hours. Dust with confectioners' sugar.

Whip the basil-infused cream in the chilled mixing bowl until soft peaks form. Fold in the sugar. Spoon or pipe the Basil Whipped Cream onto the bars before serving.

NOTE: For a fun twist on the presentation, prepare 2 batches of the bars, using lime juice and zest in place of the lemon juice and zest in the second batch. Stir in a drop of green food coloring. Cut the lemon and lime bars into squares and arrange on a serving plate in a checkerboard pattern.

Yield: 2 to 3 dozen

Molasses Spice Crisps

2 cups all-purpose flour
2 teaspoons baking soda
1 1/4 teaspoons ground cloves
1 1/4 teaspoons ground ginger
1 1/2 teaspoons ground cinnamon
1/4 teaspoon salt

1/2 cup solid butter-flavored shortening
1 cup butter, softened
3/4 cup sugar
1/4 cup packed brown sugar
1 egg
1/4 cup unsulfured molasses

Combine the flour, baking soda, cloves, ginger, cinnamon and salt in a bowl; whisk to mix. Combine the shortening, butter, sugar and brown sugar in a mixing bowl. Beat with the paddle attachment at medium speed for 2 minutes or until light and fluffy. Beat in the egg and molasses. Add the flour mixture and beat at low speed until blended. Shape into balls using a cookie scoop or small ice cream scoop. Roll each ball between the palms of your hands until smooth. Coat with additional sugar. Arrange 2 inches apart on greased cookie sheets. Bake at 375 degrees for 5 minutes and rotate the cookie sheets. Bake for 7 minutes or until set in the center and cracked around the edges. Cool on the cookie sheets on a wire rack for 5 minutes. Remove the cookies to the wire rack to cool completely. Store in an airtight container for up to 1 week.

Yield: 2 dozen

Swedish Sour Cream Cookies

2 cups sugar
1 cup shortening
2 eggs
1 cup sour cream

1 teaspoon vanilla extract
6 cups all-purpose flour
1 teaspoon baking soda
1/2 teaspoon salt

Cream the sugar and shortening in a mixing bowl until light and fluffy. Beat in the eggs, sour cream and vanilla. Add a mixture of the flour, baking soda and salt; mix well. Roll out 1/4 inch thick on a lightly floured surface. Cut out with cookie cutters. Arrange on a cookie sheet. Bake at 375 degrees for 8 to 10 minutes or until set and brown around the edges. Cool on the cookie sheets on a wire rack for 5 minutes. Remove the cookies to the wire rack to cool completely.

Yield: 6 dozen

Oatmeal Cookies

This recipe comes from Kristi and Larry Fedora. Larry is the head football coach at the University of North Carolina at Chapel Hill. His wife, Kristi, says: "These don't last long because Larry and all the kids devour them so fast."

1 cup sugar	2 cups old-fashioned oats
1 cup packed brown sugar	1 1/2 cups all-purpose flour
1 cup shortening	1 teaspoon ground cinnamon
2 eggs	1 teaspoon baking soda
1 teaspoon vanilla extract	1/2 teaspoon salt

Cream the sugar, brown sugar and shortening in a mixing bowl until light and fluffy. Beat in the eggs and vanilla. Add a mixture of the oats, flour, cinnamon, baking soda and salt gradually, beating well after each addition. Drop by tablespoonfuls onto a cookie sheet. Bake at 350 degrees for 10 minutes. Cool on the cookie sheets on a wire rack for 5 minutes. Remove the cookies to the wire rack to cool completely.

Yield: 2 dozen

Pecan Cookies

3/4 cup butter, softened	1 teaspoon baking soda
1 cup light brown sugar	1/2 teaspoon ground cinnamon
1 egg	1/4 teaspoon ground ginger
1 teaspoon vanilla extract	1/4 teaspoon salt
2 cups all-purpose flour	1 cup chopped pecans

Cream the butter, brown sugar, egg and vanilla in a mixing bowl until light and fluffy. Fold in a mixture of the flour, baking soda, cinnamon, ginger and salt; do not overmix. Fold in the pecans. Chill in the refrigerator until firm. Shape into balls. Arrange on an ungreased cookie sheet. Bake at 350 degrees for 15 minutes or until the centers are cooked through but still soft. Cool on the cookie sheets on a wire rack for 5 minutes. Remove the cookies to the wire rack to cool completely.

Yield: 2 dozen

Junior League Sugar Cookies

1 cup butter or margarine, softened
1 cup sugar
1 large egg
1 teaspoon vanilla extract
2 3/4 cups all-purpose flour
2 teaspoons baking powder

Cream the butter and sugar in a mixing bowl until light and fluffy. Add the egg and vanilla; mix well. Add a mixture of the flour and baking powder gradually, mixing well after each addition. Roll out to desired thickness on a lightly floured surface. Cut out using a 2 1/2-inch heart-shaped cookie cutter. Arrange on a cookie sheet. Bake at 400 degrees for 7 to 10 minutes or just until cookies are light brown around the edges. Cool on the cookie sheets on a wire rack for 5 minutes. Remove the cookies to the wire rack to cool completely.

Yield: 2 dozen

KEY LIME PIE MARTINI

This martini is perfectly paired for a cookie swap or dessert party. The mild sugar cookies are always a great hit with this tart drink. Combine ice, 2 ounces Licor 43, 1 ounce Key West lime juice, 1 ounce half-and-half, 1/2 teaspoon vanilla extract, and 1 ounce simple syrup (2 parts sugar with 1 part water) in a martini shaker and shake, shake, shake. Pour into martini glasses rimmed with the juice of 1 lime and sugar or finely crushed graham crackers. Garnish with whipped cream and a slice of lime. Must use Licor 43—no substitutes.

Sunshine Cookies

COOKIES

1 cup butter or margarine, softened	2 eggs
1 1/2 cups sugar	2 1/2 cups all-purpose flour
2 teaspoons grated orange peel	2 teaspoons baking powder
2 teaspoons grated lemon peel	1 teaspoon salt
1 teaspoon orange juice	3 tablespoons milk
1 teaspoon lemon juice	1 1/2 cups quick-cooking or old-fashioned oats

ORANGE LEMON GLAZE

1 tablespoon orange juice	1/2 teaspoon grated lemon peel
1 tablespoons lemon juice	3/4 cup sifted confectioners' sugar
1/2 teaspoon grated orange peel	

For the Cookies, cream the butter, sugar, orange peel, lemon peel, orange juice and lemon juice in a mixing bowl until light and fluffy. Add the eggs, one at a time, beating well after each addition. Add a mixture of the flour, baking powder and salt gradually, beating well after each addition. Beat in the milk. Fold in the oats. Drop by teaspoonfuls 2 inches apart onto greased cookie sheets. Bake at 350 degrees for 12 minutes or until cookies test done. Cool on the cookie sheets on a wire rack for 5 minutes. Remove the cookies to the wire rack.

For the Orange Lemon Glaze, combine the orange juice, lemon juice, orange peel, lemon peel and confectioners' sugar in a small bowl; mix well.

Brush the cookies with the Orange Lemon Glaze.

Yield: 2 1/2 dozen

Refectory Cafe's Cranberry Apple Pie

3 pounds Gala apples, peeled,
   cut into 1/4-inch wedges
1 cup packed light brown sugar
3/4 cup sweetened dried cranberries
1/4 cup all-purpose flour
1 teaspoon ground cinnamon
1 (9-inch) pie shell
2 tablespoons butter, melted
Pie pastry (optional)

Combine the apples, brown sugar, cranberries, flour and cinnamon in a large bowl; toss to coat the apples. Spoon into the pie shell. Drizzle with the butter. Top with additional pie pastry if desired, sealing edges and cutting vents. Bake at 350 degrees for 1 hour and 10 minutes or until the juices are thick and bubbly and the pie shell is golden brown. Shield the edges of the pie shell with foil during the last 30 minutes of baking time if needed to prevent excessive browning. Cool on a wire rack.

Yield: 6 servings

Peanut Butter Chocolate Pie

3/4 cup confectioners' sugar
1 cup reduced-fat creamy peanut butter
8 ounces 1/3-less-fat cream cheese, softened
1 (14-ounce) can sweetened condensed milk
12 ounces frozen fat-free whipped topping, thawed
2 (6-ounce) reduced-fat chocolate pie shells
2 teaspoons fat-free chocolate sundae syrup (optional)

Combine the confectioners' sugar, peanut butter and cream cheese in a large mixing bowl. Beat at medium speed until smooth. Add the sweetened condensed milk and beat until blended. Fold in the whipped topping. Spoon into the pie shells. Chill for 8 hours or until set. (Pie filling will have a soft, fluffy texture.) Freeze overnight. Drizzle each serving with chocolate syrup.

Yield: 12 servings

Carolina Moon Pie Ice Cream Pie

Moon Pies (traditional chocolate), chopped
Ice cream of choice, softened
1 graham cracker pie shell
Chopped pecans
Chocolate sundae syrup

Combine the Moon Pies and ice cream in a large bowl; mix lightly. Spoon into the pie shell. Sprinkle with pecans. Drizzle with the chocolate syrup. Freeze until serving time. May also use fruit toppings and any flavor of sundae syrup.

Yield: 6 servings

Coach K's Pumpkin Chiffon Pie

This is a favorite of Mike Krzyzewski, head coach of the Duke Men's Basketball Team, and his family. His daughter, Jamie, says: "Pumpkin Chiffon Pie is a favorite, and though it takes a while to make, is well worth the trouble. The making of this pie kicks off the K-Family Holiday Season. We have a rule that you can only listen to Christmas music when you begin cooking for the holidays. Since we all love listening to our favorite songs during this season, making the pie does not seem like a chore. When the whole gang arrives at the house, the aroma from the kitchen is familiar and enticing. The music is playing (we usually start off with the John Denver/Muppets Christmas album), the kids are excited, the turkey is in the oven, and we are all looking forward to Pumpkin Chiffon Pie for dessert."

4 envelopes unflavored gelatin	3 cups milk
2 cups sugar	8 egg yolks, lightly beaten
2 teaspoons salt	4 cups canned pumpkin
2 teaspoons ground cinnamon	8 egg whites
2 teaspoons allspice	1 cup sugar
1 teaspoon ground ginger	2 cups heavy whipping cream, whipped
1 teaspoon ground nutmeg	4 (9-inch) graham cracker pie shells

Put on a holiday apron and your favorite Christmas music. Combine the gelatin, 2 cups sugar, salt, cinnamon, allspice, ginger and nutmeg in a large saucepan. Stir in the milk, egg yolks and pumpkin. Bring to a boil over medium heat, stirring constantly to dissolve the gelatin. Cool for several minutes. Chill until partially set; do not chill too long or the filling will become too firm. Beat the egg whites in a large mixing bowl until soft peaks form. Add 1 cup sugar gradually, beating constantly. Beat until stiff peaks form. Fold the beaten egg whites and whipped cream into the pumpkin mixture until blended. Spoon into the pie shells. Chill until firm. Serve with additional whipped cream if desired.

Yield: 24 servings

Southern Pecan Pie

1/3 cup margarine
1/2 cup packed light brown sugar
3 eggs, lightly beaten
1 cup light corn syrup
1 teaspoon vanilla extract
1 cup chopped pecans
1 unbaked pie shell

Cream the margarine and brown sugar in a mixing bowl until light and fluffy. Add the eggs and mix well. Add the corn syrup, vanilla and pecans; mix well. Pour into the pie shell. Bake at 450 degrees for 10 minutes; reduce the oven temperature to 350 degrees. Bake for 45 to 50 minutes longer or until set.

Yield: 6 servings

PECAN VS. PECAN PRONUNCIATION

Are they "pee-cans" or "pah-cahns"? Do you pronounce it differently when referring to the name of a praline or a pie? After much research, it actually does not matter what region of the state you live in, and it's not even Northern versus Southern. It all comes down to urban versus rural! If you want to sound a little more country, go with "pee-can," but if you would like to sound more urbane, go with "pah-cahn." Either way you say it, they are delicious!

Piedmont's Ten Dollar Pie

A "Ten Dollar Pie" isn't a pie at all, but is actually a cobbler originating in the lowcountry area of South Carolina. Named for its standard price at market, this Ten Dollar Pie recipe has a long history in Piedmont Executive Chef Ben Adams' family.

2 cups peeled, coarsely chopped pears
2 cups peeled, coarsely chopped apples
3 tablespoons ground cinnamon
Pinch of salt
1/4 cup (about) sugar
1 cup all-purpose flour
1 cup sugar
1 tablespoon baking powder
1 cup milk
1/2 cup butter

Combine the pears, apples, cinnamon, salt and 1/4 cup sugar, or enough to bring out the natural sweetness of the fruit, in a sauté pan and sauté just until crisp-tender; do not overcook.

Combine the flour, 1 cup sugar and baking powder in a bowl and mix well. Add the milk gradually, whisking until smooth. Place the butter in a soufflé dish or deep baking dish. Bake at 360 to 365 degrees until melted and lightly browned. Pour the batter into the soufflé dish. Spoon the fruit evenly over the batter. Bake for 15 minutes or until the crust is golden brown.

Yield: 6 servings

PIEDMONT RESTAURANT

Piedmont Restaurant focuses on adventurous, seasonal cooking, inspired by all that the Piedmont region of North Carolina has to offer. Known for using local, farm-grown ingredients and avant-garde methods, Piedmont works to create classic dishes that are "reimagined," resulting in truly flavorful, comforting food. Piedmont's craft cocktails, local beers, and versatile wine list complete the modern farm-to-table experience.

Blueberry Peach Cobbler with Berry Whipped Cream

COBBLER

4 medium peaches, peeled and
   very thinly sliced, or unpeeled organic
   peaches, thinly sliced
1/2 cup sugar
4 tablespoons butter
Pinch of coarse sea salt
1 cup whole organic oats
   (not quick-cooking oats)
3 tablespoons buttermilk
1 cup ground oats or all-purpose flour

1 cup turbinado sugar
1 teaspoon baking powder
1 teaspoon grated lemon zest
1 teaspoon ground cinnamon
1 cup fresh blueberries
1 tablespoon honey
4 tablespoons butter, melted
2 teaspoons vanilla extract
1 teaspoon cornstarch
Juice of 1 small lemon

BERRY WHIPPED CREAM

1 cup strawberries
1/2 tablespoon confectioners' sugar
1 cup heavy whipping cream

1 tablespoon confectioners' sugar
1 teaspoon vanilla extract

For the Cobbler, combine the peaches and 1/2 cup sugar in a bowl and mix gently. Add the peach mixture to 4 tablespoons butter and salt in a saucepan. Cook over low heat until the peaches are tender and the juices are slightly thickened, stirring frequently. Combine the whole oats and buttermilk in a bowl; mix well. Let stand for 10 minutes. Combine the ground oats, turbinado sugar, baking powder, lemon zest and cinnamon in a blender and process until smooth. Add to the whole oats mixture and mix well. Toss the blueberries with the honey. Spoon into the bottom of a greased pie plate. Add the peaches and half the peach liquid. Combine 4 tablespoons butter and remaining peach liquid in a small bowl. Stir in the vanilla, cornstarch and lemon juice. Add to the oats mixture and mix well. Add additional oats if the mixture is too thin. Spread over the fruit mixture. Bake at 350 degrees for 30 to 35 minutes or until the cobbler begins to bubble and the topping is golden brown. Let stand for 15 minutes to cool.

For the Berry Whipped Cream, combine the strawberries and 1/2 tablespoon confectioners' sugar in a blender and process until puréed. Whip the whipping cream, 1 tablespoon confectioners' sugar and vanilla in a bowl until soft peaks form. Swirl the strawberry purée into the whipped cream.

Serve the cobbler warm with Berry Whipped Cream or ice cream.

Yield: 6 servings

Caramel Apple Dip with Chapel Hill Toffee

1 cup packed brown sugar
1/2 cup half-and-half
4 tablespoons butter
Pinch of salt
1 tablespoon vanilla extract
8 ounces cream cheese
10 to 12 ounces Chapel Hill Toffee crumbles
8 to 10 Granny Smith or Red Delicious apples,
   or a mixture of both, sliced

Combine the brown sugar, half-and-half, butter and salt in a saucepan. Cook over medium-low heat for 5 minutes or until thickened, gently whisking constantly. Stir in the vanilla. Combine the warm sauce and cream cheese in a blender and process until smooth. Pour into a dish or deep platter. Sprinkle with the toffee. Serve with the apples.

NOTE: When preparing apples ahead of serving time, soak in pineapple juice to prevent browning. Lemon juice will also work, but it may make the Granny Smith apples too tart.

Yield: about 2 cups

CHAPEL HILL TOFFEE

"For as long as we can remember, our mom has been making delicious, homemade toffee. In 2006, after years of perfecting her recipe, Chapel Hill Toffee was officially born! Today, we still make our toffee using pecans and dark chocolate right here in the 'Southern Part of Heaven.' We hope you enjoy!"

—The Graves Family

Southern-Style Banana Pudding

3/4 cup sugar
4 tablespoons cornstarch
3 1/2 cups whole milk
1 vanilla bean, sliced lengthwise and
    seeded
5 egg yolks, lightly beaten
5 tablespoons unsalted butter

4 egg whites
1/4 teaspoon cream of tartar
1/3 cup superfine sugar
5 medium bananas, sliced
1 (12-ounce) package vanilla wafers, or
    Homemade Vanilla Wafers (recipe below)

Combine the sugar and cornstarch in a double boiler over simmering water; mix well. Add the milk gradually, stirring constantly. Add the vanilla bean pod and seeds. Stir a small amount of the hot custard into the egg yolks in a bowl to temper. Add the egg yolks to the hot custard, stirring constantly. Cook for 2 minutes, stirring constantly; remove from the heat. Discard the vanilla pod. Add the butter and cook until melted, stirring constantly. Let stand to cool. Beat the egg whites and cream of tartar in a mixing bowl until soft peaks form. Add the superfine sugar gradually, beating constantly until very stiff peaks form. Alternate layers of pudding, bananas and vanilla wafers in a 9 x 9-inch baking dish, beginning and ending with pudding. Top with the meringue. Bake at 350 degrees for 15 minutes or until the meringue is golden brown. Serve hot or cold.

Yield: 6 to 8 servings

Homemade Vanilla Wafers

1/2 cup butter, softened
1 cup sugar
1 egg
1 tablespoon vanilla extract

1 1/3 cups all-purpose flour
3/4 teaspoon baking powder
1/4 teaspoon kosher salt

Cream the butter and sugar in a large mixing bowl until light and fluffy. Beat in the egg and vanilla. Add a mixture of the flour, baking powder and salt gradually, beating well after each addition. Drop by teaspoonfuls 2 inches apart onto ungreased cookie sheets. Bake at 350 degrees for 12 to 15 minutes or until the edges of the cookies are golden brown. Cool on wire racks.

Yield: 3 1/2 to 4 dozen

Pumpkin Pie Dip

8 ounces cream cheese, softened
2 cups confectioners' sugar
1 (15-ounce) can pumpkin
1/2 cup sour cream

1 teaspoon ground cinnamon
1 teaspoon pumpkin pie spice
1/2 teaspoon ground ginger

Combine the cream cheese and confectioners' sugar in a large mixing bowl. Beat until smooth and blended. Add the pumpkin, sour cream, cinnamon, pumpkin pie spice and ginger gradually, beating until smooth after each addition. Serve with gingersnaps or apples, or your favorite cookies or fruit.

Yield: 5 to 6 cups

Chocolate Delight

3/4 cup margarine, melted
1 1/2 cups flour
8 ounces cream cheese, softened
32 ounces frozen whipped topping, thawed

1 cup confectioners' sugar
3 cups whole milk
2 (3-ounce) packages instant chocolate pudding mix
Chopped pecans

Combine the margarine and flour in a bowl; mix with hands until crumbly. Press over the bottom of a greased 9 x 13-inch baking dish. Bake at 350 degrees for 20 to 30 minutes or until browned. Cool for 1 hour. Combine the cream cheese, half the whipped topping and the confectioners' sugar in a large bowl; mix well using a spoon. Spread over the cooled crust. Combine the milk and chocolate pudding mix in a mixing bowl and beat until thickened. Spread over the cream cheese layer. Spread the remaining whipped topping over the pudding. Sprinkle with pecans. Chill until serving time.

Yield: 8 to 12 servings

Crème Brûlée

4 cups whole milk
1/2 cup sugar
1 vanilla bean, split and seeds removed
6 large eggs, beaten
2/3 cup sugar

Combine the milk, 1/2 cup sugar and vanilla bean seeds in a bowl; mix well. Pour into a large saucepan. Add the vanilla bean pod. Cook over medium-low heat until the sugar is dissolved, stirring constantly; discard the vanilla bean pod. Beat the eggs in a mixing bowl until frothy. Add the milk mixture to the eggs very gradually, stirring constantly to prevent "cooking" the eggs. Spoon into small ramekins or crème brûlée dishes. Place in a large baking dish. Using a teakettle, fill the larger dish with enough water to reach halfway up the sides of the ramekins to make a water bath. Bake at 350 degrees for 1 hour or until the tops are lightly browned and of custard consistency. Let stand until completely cooled. Chill overnight. Sprinkle the tops with 2/3 cup sugar. Brûlée the sugar using a torch.

Yield: 6 servings

HOW TO BRÛLÉE

To brûlée literally means "to burn" in French. You will need a butane culinary torch available at most culinary supply stores. Let the chilled custard stand until at room temperature. Pat the tops gently with paper towels to remove any moisture. Sprinkle with enough sugar to make a thin layer; shake off any excess. Apply a medium flame with the butane torch, moving over the sugar constantly until covered with a caramel-colored glaze. Let stand for 30 seconds or until hardened.

Pita Mizithra

6 eggs, beaten
1 1/2 cups sugar
1 tablespoon uncooked farina or grits
15 ounces ricotta cheese

10 to 12 sheets phyllo
Melted butter
Cinnamon sugar to taste

Beat the eggs, sugar and farina in a large mixing bowl until light and fluffy. Fold in the ricotta using a spoon. Line a buttered shallow 8 x 8-inch baking pan with 5 or 6 sheets of phyllo, brushing each layer with butter. Spread with the ricotta mixture. Top with the remaining sheets of phyllo, brushing each layer with butter. Bake at 350 degrees for 50 to 55 minutes. Sprinkle with cinnamon sugar. Let stand to cool.

Yield: 4 to 6 servings

Pumpkin Tiramisu

1 1/2 cups whipping cream
3/4 cup sugar
1 (5-ounce) can pumpkin
8 ounces mascarpone cheese

1 teaspoon pumpkin pie spice
36 ladyfingers
5 tablespoons dark rum
1 cup crushed amaretti cookies

Combine the whipping cream and sugar in a large mixing bowl. Beat until soft peaks form. Beat in the pumpkin, mascarpone cheese and pumpkin pie spice. Line the bottom of a 9-inch springform pan with half the ladyfingers. Sprinkle with half the rum. Spread with half the pumpkin mixture. Repeat the layers with the remaining ladyfingers, rum and pumpkin mixture. Chill overnight. Sprinkle the amaretti cookies over the top just before serving.

Yield: 8 servings

Slow Cooker Apple Crisp

APPLE FILLING

Nonstick cooking spray
3 tablespoons sugar
2 tablespoons packed brown sugar
1 1/2 teaspoons all-purpose flour
1/2 teaspoon ground cinnamon
1/2 teaspoon ground nutmeg

1/8 teaspoon allspice
1/8 teaspoon ground ginger
1/4 cup water
4 1/2 to 5 cups peeled chopped apples,
   such as 3 large Honeycrisp apples

CRISP TOPPING

1/2 cup flour
1/4 cup packed brown sugar
2 tablespoons sugar
1/4 cup chopped nuts

1/2 cup oats
1/8 teaspoon baking powder
1/8 teaspoon baking soda
4 tablespoons butter, melted

For the Apple Filling, spray the slow cooker with nonstick cooking spray. Mix the sugar, brown sugar, flour, cinnamon, nutmeg, allspice, ginger and water in a large bowl. Add the apples, tossing to coat. Pour into the prepared slow cooker.

For the Crisp Topping, combine the flour, brown sugar, sugar, nuts, oats, baking powder and baking soda in a bowl; mix well. Add the butter, stirring to make a crumbly mixture. Sprinkle over the apples; cover. Cook on High for 2 to 3 hours or on Low for 4 to 5 hours. Serve warm topped with good vanilla ice cream if desired.

Yield: 6 to 8 servings

VIETRI
IRRESISTIBLY ITALIAN

Susan Gravely's
Simple Tips for Entertaining

Susan Gravely grew up in the South, where porches wrapped around the house, lightning bugs illuminated the night sky, dinner parties filled the calendar, and visitors were always welcome. Susan and her sister, Frances, remember well the careful preparation behind a special evening, and they were often asked to help set the table. Little did Susan know that very chore would turn into her life's passion. Today, Susan is CEO and founder of VIETRI, the 31-year-old Hillsborough-based lifestyle brand of Italian artisan-crafted dinnerware (featured in this cookbook) and home and garden décor. Over the years, she has perfected her formula for easy, gracious entertaining.

1. I love hosting gatherings spontaneously. People love to be together, and they love a nice glass of wine; so as long you bring the two together, you're bound for a good time.

2. To that point, no one knows if your original plan is going as expected, so relax! Your harried or anxious feelings will rub off on your guests. Enjoy yourself and your guests will enjoy themselves, too.

3. Don't worry if all the preparations for dinner aren't ready when guests arrive. My entertaining style is casual, so I invite friends into the kitchen to chat while I'm attending to the final touches.

4. Music adds so much! Put a favorite album or playlist on that sounds great in the background.

5. Bring the outside in. I cut greenery from the garden, and I arrange it with flowers. The leaf smell is so fresh, and it's an especially nice touch in colder months.

6. When entertaining large groups, have guests make themselves a nametag when they come in. I like to ask guests to write a fun fact or how they know the host so that it's easier for them to meet others.

7. Make your table a conversation piece. Of course, I entertain on VIETRI, and I love that our beautiful collections inspire discussions about craftsmanship, Italy, and good living.

8. Serve delicious, simple food. For an appetizer, I pick up prosciutto, good cheeses, and bread from the farmer's market. I add a bit of pear preserves to spread with the cheeses as a special touch.

9. For dinner, a chili or vegetable soup and salad is comforting and easy. A cold soup and bread with fresh green salad is refreshing for summer. I like to serve things that are colorful.

10. I generally conclude a meal with fruit-based desserts. They cleanse the palate, and I appreciate that they don't need much sugar. For your chocolate addicts, have a small plate of chocolates to pass around.

11. After eating, my husband and I often suggest a walk around the neighborhood or another activity. We always have a great time on the bocce court in our garden, especially when the competition gets fierce!

12. The most important thing is to relax. Entertaining should not be a daunting or nerve-racking experience. Enjoy spending time with your family and friends!

Grilling 101

Too often, cooks just throw food on the grill and hope for the best.
With only a few essential techniques, you can be a grill master.

Charcoal vs. Gas: Which kind of grill is better? It is not really a question of quality, but convenience. Charcoal adds that inimitable smoky taste to grilled meats, whereas it's easier to turn on the gas grill. The choice is yours; serious grillers have both!

Direct and Indirect Heat: How food is positioned over the heat source affects cooking. Direct cooking is cooking food directly over hot coals or the burners of a gas grill. This is reserved for food that will cook in about 20 minutes, such as burgers, steaks, boneless chicken, and frankfurters. Indirect cooking refers to placing food away from the heat source so it cooks by radiated heat. Some foods may be seared over direct heat first before being moved to the cool side of the grill to cook by indirect heat. This method is reserved for large cuts of meat—roasts, bone-in or whole chicken, and ribs.

Barbecuing is cooking with indirect heat while adding smoke provided by wood chunks or chips that have been soaked in cold water (for at least 30 minutes) and drained. Wood chunks work best with charcoal; add them to the charcoal before lighting. Or you can simply sprinkle drained wood chips over the coals. For a gas grill, use wood chips placed in a metal smoker box recommended by your grill's manufacturer. Start with dry chips in the box, let them ignite, and then add drained wood chips.

Using Lump Charcoal: The Fresh Market sells natural lump charcoal without additives. It burns at a higher temperature than briquettes and doesn't have the additives that cause "off" odors. A charcoal chimney with newspaper crumpled in the bottom is the best way to start the first coals. Mound more charcoal over the lighted coals, and let the coals burn until they are covered with white ash. Spread the charcoal in the grill, but leave a 4-inch perimeter around the coals for direct heat so you have a place to move the food when it drips its fat. The coals should be on one side of the grill for indirect heat. Charcoal burns hottest during the first 20 minutes, then drops heat rapidly. With indirect heat, you will have to add a few lumps to the coals every half hour to keep the coals going.

Know Your Heat: High heat is 450 degrees Fahrenheit and above, medium heat is 350 to 450 degrees, and low heat is 275 to 350 degrees. It is easy to adjust the heat on gas grills, as most of them have thermometers in their lids that can be regulated with a twist of a knob. You can also place an oven thermometer in the grill. The heat in a charcoal grill can be changed by the amount of coals used (lots of charcoal for high heat and less for lower temperatures). To check an accurate reading in a charcoal grill, drop a candy thermometer through the top vent of the lid.

Keep the Lid On: Fire needs oxygen to stay alive, so a closed lid reduces the chances of flare-ups, most of which are caused by fat or marinade dripping from the food onto the heat source. If you have a charcoal grill, the vents on the lid and underneath the kettle can be opened or shut to control the air flow. For high heat, keep the vents wide open to feed the flame. For medium heat, close them halfway to reduce the oxygen so the fire burns at a lower temperature. Close the vents only when you want to cut off the oxygen completely to shut the grill down.

Taste of Tobacco Road
Cookbook Development Team

Junior League of Durham and Orange Counties
Board of Directors

Candace Anderson, Meghan Blackledge, Halley Bogart, Stephanie Brennan,
Jane Bullock, Nakira Carter, Arielle Cutrara, Jessica Dedrick, Laura Dickerson, Lauren Dickerson,
Susan Easterling, Lauren Lawrence, Jennifer Horner, Lisa Johnson, Laura Klas, Kim Leder,
Betsy Lovell, Kristina Magnuson, Kristyn Monaghan, Kelly Owens, Kate Price,
Michele Reister, Shamieka Rhinehart, Stephanie Robinette, Jen Rosen, Kate Rugani,
Morgan Rutherford, Alivia Sholtz, Megan Skidmore, Jordan Thorndyke, Anna Walker,
Christina Webb, Jessica Whilden, Julie Williams, Lauren Zedek

Cookbook Leadership Committee

Margret Anne Hutaff, Sarah Graham Motsinger, Ashley Ray Utz

Marie-Angela Kikuchi, Amy Loochtan, Kara Pittman, Nicole Steck, Cole Taylor

Cookbook Committee

Katie Atkins, Katie Barrett, Meg Beal, Amber Berry, Meghan Blackledge,
Katie Bowden, Anne-Marie Cummings, Siobahn Day, Emily Egge, Alexis Gaines,
Shannon Gatlin, Vanessa Green, Rachel Groce, Ashley Hale, Lindsay Hiatt,
Cameron Jordan, Kate Price, Culver Scales, Elizabeth Fawcett Smith, Jamie Mae Smith,
Lucy Taylor, Candace Winkler, Mary-Kelsey Wrenn

JUNIOR LEAGUE OF
DURHAM AND ORANGE COUNTIES
Women building better communities®

Contributors

Taste of Tobacco Road is a collection of over 150 recipes that showcase the local flair and flavors of our favorite place to call home. We would like to express our sincere gratitude to the following individuals who have let us into their homes by sharing favorite family recipes and stories:

Amy Akers	Mary Cook Fawcett	Kim Leder	Kate Rugani
Candace Anderson	Christi Fedora	Samantha Leder	Katherine Runnels
Chilon Anderson	Bentley Fisher	Jenny Levy	Culver Scales
Nancy Anderson	Dana Fox	Amy Loochtan	Ashley Hibbard Scallion
Alison Arnold	Meredith Fulton	Adam Lunger	Megan Skidmore
Katie Atkins	Alexis Gaines	Catherine Lunger	Elizabeth Fawcett Smith
Chelsea Avery	Kelly Garcia	Laura Tomasulo Magid	Jamie Smith
Katie Barrett	Shannon Gatlin	Connie Mahan	Susan Smith
Meg Beal	Stephanie Glover	Beth Maxwell	Jamie Krzyzewski Spatola
Amber Berry	Cara Goodwin	Catherine McCalley	Susan Spratt
Laura Biediger	Sally Graham	Kathy McPherson	Nicole Steck
Lindsay Bipes	Vanessa Green	Kristyn Monaghan	Cathleen Connell Summey
Meghan Blackledge	Britt Guarglia	Lindsay Moore	Catherine Colgate Taylor
Halley Bogart	Betty Ann Guidry	Sarah Graham Motsinger	Kate McAllister Taylor
Katie Bowden	Carrie Sweet Harbinson	Courtney Mumford	Lucy Taylor
Eleanor Dreher Boyd	Kate Harshbarger	Erin Nolen	Anna Thompson
Courtney Brown	Bryan Hassin	Susan O'Connor	Jordan Thorndyke
Jane Bullock	Sylvia Hatchell	Kelly Owens	Terri Reynolds Tolley
Nakira Carter	Lauren Havens	Ellen Parker	Jenny Blount Tucker
Julie Chase	Lindsay Hiatt	Tarry Payton	Shannon Tucker
Alexandria Maria Cooley	Helen Barbee Higgins	Maren Penny	Ashley Ray Utz
Anne-Marie Cummings	Alexandra Holmgren	Kara Lynn Pittman	Anna Walker
Karen Cunningham	Betsy Keville Hughes	Brenda Hill Pollard	Sarah Swann Warren
Tina Cunningham	Lauren Lawrence	Sara Tatum Pottenger	Christina Webb
Arielle Cutrara	Hungry Leaf	Kelly Preussner	Jenny Weber
Sara Dawson	Meghan Hunt	Kate Price	Blair McDonald Welborn
Siobahn Day	Margret Anne Hutaff	Bridgett Higgins Ray	Jessica Crowe Whilden
Jessica Dedrick	Susan East Hutaff	Michele Reister	Candace Michelle Winkler
Lauren Olivia Dickerson	Emily Johnson	Elizabeth Martin Richards	Brittni Mattocks Winslow
Mandy Dickerson	Lisa Johnson	Jenny Robbins	Sarah Woodard
Anson Dorrance	Marie-Angela Kikuchi	Codruta Roberts	Jessica Woolridge
Jean Durham	Laura Klas	Stephanie Robinette	Stacey Yusko
Susan Easterling	Katherine Lamberth	Susan Ross	Lauren Zedek
Crystal Ebert	Lauren Lawrence	Jane Royall	

Index

Taste of Tobacco Road
A Culinary Journey Along the Famous Nine Miles

Food Photography: Anna Routh Photography, Chapel Hill, North Carolina
Food Styling: Alex Blake, Buttermilk Creative, Greensboro, North Carolina

Special Appreciation
Local Area Photography: Roy Rice Photography, Chapel Hill, North Carolina
Photography Location: Home of Sally Graham, JLDOC Sustainer
Editing Assistance: Kathy McPherson, JLDOC Sustainer and Past President
Foreword: Sara Foster, Foster's Market
Special thanks to all of our members who submitted, cooked, and tested each recipe,
and collaborated with the production of *Taste of Tobacco Road*.

The Junior League of Durham and Orange Counties, Inc., is an organization of women
committed to promoting voluntarism, developing the potential of women, and improving communities through the
effective action and leadership of trained volunteers. Its purpose is exclusively educational and charitable.

This cookbook is a collection of favorite recipes, which are not necessarily original recipes.

Library of Congress Control Number: 2015952306
ISBN: 978-0-9615845-2-8

Edited, Designed, and Manufactured by

Favorite Recipes® Press
An imprint of

SOUTHWESTERN Publishing Group®

P.O. Box 305142
Nashville, Tennessee 37230
1-800-358-0560

Project Manager: Sheila Thomas   Designer: Steve Newman
Editor: Mary Cummings   Proofreader: Linda Brock

Manufactured in the United States of America
First Printing: November 2015

The Famous Nine Miles

WAKE FOREST
UNIVERSITY

Chapel Hill

Carrboro

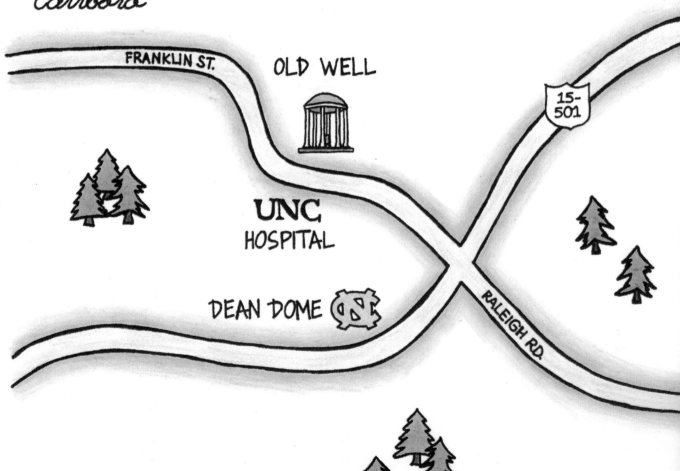

FRANKLIN ST.

OLD WELL

15-
501

UNC
HOSPITAL

DEAN DOME

RALEIGH RD.